EXTREME LOGIC PUZZLES

BARRY R. CLARKE

**PUZZLE
WRIGHT
PRESS**
New York

PUZZLE WRIGHT PRESS

New York

An Imprint of Sterling Publishing
1166 Avenue of the Americas
New York, NY 10036

Text © 2015 by Barry R. Clarke
Illustrations © 2015 by Sterling Publishing

Illustrated by Rob Collinet

ISBN 978-1-4549-0993-4

Distributed in Canada by Sterling Publishing
C/o Canadian Manda Group, 664 Annette Street
Toronto, Ontario, Canada M6S 2C8
Distributed in the United Kingdom by GMC Distribution Services
Castle Place, 166 High Street, Lewes, East Sussex, England BN7 1XU
Distributed in Australia by Capricorn Link (Australia) Pty. Ltd.
P.O. Box 704, Windsor, NSW 2756, Australia

For information about custom editions, special sales, and premium and
corporate purchases, please contact Sterling Special Sales at 800-805-5489 or
specialsales@sterlingpublishing.com.

Manufactured in Canada

2   4   6   8   10   9   7   5   3   1

www.puzzlewright.com

Contents

Introduction

My previous book, *Challenging Logic Puzzles*, has proved to be so popular that it seemed there really ought to be another one. So here it is! I've been fascinated to receive feedback on how readers have employed the puzzles from my previous collection. An elderly lady from Connecticut solves them for therapy "at least one hour a day," a mathematics teacher from Virginia has used them to train his summer school for gifted children, and there are numerous reports of them entertaining entire families. One crime author penned a scenario in which Dr. Watson presented the book to a restless Sherlock Holmes, who confidently predicted that he would complete them all in less than fifteen minutes. Not so elementary, my dear Holmes! Others have taken up the challenge with a vengeance. A computer programmer succeeded in constructing an algorithm to crack the Mix-and-Match problems (such as "Pet Peeve" on page 7 and others), and according to a puzzle enthusiast from Philadelphia, if *New York Times* crossword puzzles were an 8 then "these are an 11."

In reality, though, there is something for everyone here. As with my previous book, the puzzles gradually increase in difficulty as the pages turn, except there is now an even greater variety of puzzles! (The answers are not given in order, though, so as to help prevent solvers from accidentally seeing the answer to the next puzzle.)

Happy solving!

—Barry R. Clarke
Oxford
barryispuzzled.com

Treasure Chests

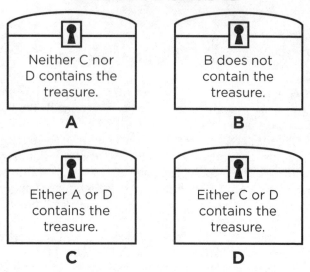

A
Neither C nor D contains the treasure.

B
B does not contain the treasure.

C
Either A or D contains the treasure.

D
Either C or D contains the treasure.

Four treasure chests each have a statement attached. Only one contains treasure. If exactly two of the four statements are false, which chest has the treasure?

Solution on page 76.

The Plumber's Apprentice

Bob the plumber's apprentice has just completed the task of connecting four taps (A, B, C, and D, from left to right) to the water mains. However, whichever tap he turns on, water always pours out of a different tap! Clearly, each tap controls one and only one of the other taps.

1) Tap A did not control tap C.
2) Tap C did not control tap D.
3) Only one of the taps did not control an adjacent tap.

For each tap, can you discover the other tap it controlled?

Solution on page 73.

Pet Peeve

	Owner's first name	Owner's last name	Pet	Pet's name
1	Jake	Kline	goat	Fred
2	Alvin	Lyne	pig	George
3	Bess	Crud	cat	Helen
4	Sid	Nose	dog	Ian
5	Trish	Dank	rabbit	Josie

The *Daily Drivel* has just published its poll to find the most annoying pet in Tiddleton. Although each entry is in the correct column, only one entry in each column is correctly positioned. The following facts are true about the correct order:

1) Ian is two places below the pig.
2) Crud is two places above Fred but one above Alvin.
3) The rabbit's name is Josie.
4) Dank is three places below the cat and one below Sid.
5) Trish is three places below Nose.

Can you find the correct owner's full name, pet, and pet's name for each position?

Solution on page 89.

Safe Cracker 1

Four different digits from 1 to 9 are required to open a safe.

1) The first digit is smaller than the second.
2) The second and third digits total 8.
3) The first and fourth digits differ by 2.
4) The third digit is greater than 5.

Can you find the four-digit combination?

Solution on page 64.

Identity Parade 1

A police artist has drawn the faces of a lineup of four female suspects seen stealing dresses from market stalls. The faces (labeled A to D) consist of four rows of hair, eyes, noses, and mouths. Although the correct features are in each row, only one of the four in each row is correctly positioned. The following facts are true about the correct order:

1) A's mouth is one place to the right of B's hair but one place to the left of D's eyes.
2) C's hair is one place to the right of her eyes but two places to the right of D's nose.
3) C's mouth is two places to the left of her nose.

Can you give the correct hair, eyes, nose, and mouth for each position?

Solution on page 70.

Alien Mutations 1

Above are nine mutation chambers labeled A to I, surrounded by alien figures. Each alien on the left has passed through the three chambers directly to its right and been transformed into the alien on the far right (e.g., the figure to the left of A has moved through chambers A, B, and C to finish as the one to the right of C). Similarly, each alien shown above the chambers has passed through the three chambers directly below to finish as seen at the bottom. Each chamber always performs a single alteration only (and each chamber must cause a change in both aliens that enter it): specifying head or body shape, adding or removing antennae, adding or removing upper or lower appendages, or specifying posture. What does each chamber do?

Solution on page 64.

Orange County Conundrum

In Orange County, California, a farmer noticed that some of his carrots had been stolen. Dibble, a police officer in the field, had received a tip-off that it was a child with red hair, so he pulled in five children fitting that description who had been seen together near the farm. Intending to get to the root of the matter he took a statement from each carrot-top teen as follows:

Arthur said, "It was Carol or Ethel."
Benny said, "It was Carol or Dave."
Carol said, "It was Benny or Dave."
Dave said, "It was Arthur or Carol."
Ethel said, "It was Arthur or Benny."

Luckily, Officer Dibble knew the children well, and knew that exactly two were habitual liars who never told the truth, while the other three always told the truth. Unfortunately, he was also bad with faces, so he didn't know which were which. Nonetheless, he managed to discover which child had been stealing the carrots. Who was lying and who had stolen the carrots?

Solution on page 84.

Magic Hats 1

There are four hats: two white and two black. Three friends, Ant, Bendy, and Cringe, are blindfolded and, in turn, a hat is placed on each person's head. The three are then arranged in a circle, the leftover hat is hidden, and the blindfolds removed so that each of the three can see the other two hats but not his own. Each is asked to make a statement about the colors of the two hats he can see. Ant says "at least one black"; Bendy reports "two white"; and Cringe states "only one black." The white hats are magic; anyone wearing a white one must tell the truth, but anyone wearing a black one may lie or tell the truth. Exactly one statement is a lie. Can you give the color hat each is wearing and name the liar?

Solution on page 68.

Unchained Melody

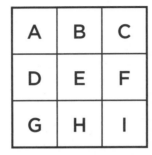

A	B	C
D	E	F
G	H	I

Nine prison cells were arranged as shown. Each contained a dangerous criminal who could hear sound from any cell immediately adjacent to his own horizontally or vertically, although not diagonally. As part of an attempt at rehabilitation, the inmates were encouraged to sing. To discover how successful the initiative was, certain prisoners were asked about the number of his neighbors that could be heard singing. Prisoner B said "one"; C said "one"; D said "two"; E said "two"; H said "one"; and I said "one."

If no row or column had three singers, which prisoners had been singing?

Solution on page 82.

Card Sharp

No more than one statement with at least two cards below it is true.

Exactly one statement is true.

The statements alternate between true and false.

There are more true statements than false statements.

Professor Neuron was interviewing candidates for the School of Logic at Perspica City University. He placed the line of four cards shown above on the table in front of his latest interviewee, Miss Take. He then invited her to decide which ones were true (if any) and which were false (if any).

If the statements are consistent, which statements are true?

Solution on page 73.

Counting Sheep 1

1	7	9	6	1	3
8	3	1	5	4	4
5	8	2	9	6	1
8	2	1	3	9	4
1	5	8	4	3	7
3	4	5	2	6	9

Above are 36 pens each containing a number of sheep. A buyer bought all the sheep in 12 of the pens. Delete two numbers from each row and column to leave 24 occupied pens so that each row and column contains 20 sheep.

Solution on page 65.

The Six Window Cleaners

On Flannel Street, six window cleaners—Alf, Bert, Colin, Doris, Ethel, and Freda—were each perched on a ladder with six rungs. No two were on the same level. Freda was below Doris, Ethel was three rungs away from Alf, Colin was at least three rungs below Bert (who was not on the top rung), and Ethel was somewhere below Colin.

Can you find the descending order of the six window cleaners?

Solution on page 78.

Birthday Brainbuster

Agatha, Bibble, Crump, and Dibdib have their birthdays in four different months. The number of letters in the four months are different consecutive numbers, such that Agatha has the month with the smallest number of letters, Bibble has the next highest, Crump the next, and Dibdib has the month with the greatest number of letters.

When recently asked by an acquaintance about their birthdays, Agatha stated that "No letter in my month appears in Bibble's month"; Bibble claimed "My month is later than Dibdib's in the calendar"; Crump said "My month has 31 days"; and Dibdib stated "My month does not have 31 days."

The trouble is, each of the four either always tells the truth or always lies, and Agatha claimed that Bibble always lies, Bibble said that Crump always tells the truth, Crump claimed that Dibdib always lies, and Dibdib maintained that Agatha always tells the truth.

In what months do Agatha, Bibble, Crump, and Dibdib have their birthdays?

Solution on page 87.

Alien Mutations 2

Above are nine mutation chambers labeled A to I, surrounded by alien figures. Each alien on the left has passed through the three chambers directly to its right and been transformed into the alien on the far right (e.g., the figure to the left of A has moved through chambers A, B, and C to finish as the one to the right of C). Similarly, each alien shown above the chambers has passed through the three chambers directly below to finish as seen at the bottom. Each chamber always performs a single alteration only (and each chamber must cause a change in both aliens that enter it): specifying head or body shape, adding or removing antennae, adding or removing upper or lower appendages, or specifying posture. What does each chamber do?

Solution on page 75.

Right on Queue

Six children were standing in a queue at a candy store. They had the following amounts of money: Andy had $3, Barbara had $5, Colin had $9, Doris had $10, Ethel had $11, and Fred had $15. The following conditions applied to their places in the queue:

1) The second and fifth place total was divisible by eight.
2) The third and fourth place total was a prime number.
3) The first and fifth place total was divisible by six.
4) The second and third place total was the same as the fifth and sixth place total.

Can you place the six children in the correct order in the queue?

Solution on page 67.

Safe Cracker 2

Four different digits from 1 to 9 are required to open a safe.

1) The first digit is greater than the second.
2) The second and third digits total 13.
3) The first and second digits differ by 3.
4) The third and fourth digits differ by 2.

Can you find the four-digit combination?

Solution on page 65.

Identity Parade 2

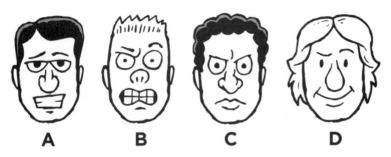

A   **B**   **C**   **D**

Tiny Tom was asked to draw in a line the faces (labeled A to D) of the four military action figures he had just looked at in the department store. The faces he drew consist of four rows of hair, eyes, noses, and mouths. Although the correct features are in each row, only one of the four in each row is correctly positioned. The following facts are true about the correct order:

1) C's eyes are one place to the left of his mouth.
2) B's mouth is not next to C's mouth.
3) A's nose is one place to the left of D's hair.
4) B's eyes are not with C's mouth but are one place to the right of B's hair.
5) B's nose is one place to the right of his mouth.

Can you find the correct hair, eyes, nose, and mouth for each position?

Solution on page 95.

The Principal's Cadillac

Six pupils from the local high school were being interviewed about who spray-painted the principal's Cadillac. Each made a statement about a set of three pupils of the six that contained the culprit. However, exactly two statements were lies.

Aimless said, "It was Clod, Earwig, or Flopwit."
Bibble said, "It was Clod, Dimple, or me."
Clod said, "It was Aimless, Dimple, or me."
Dimple said, "It was Aimless, Earwig, or me."
Earwig said, "It was Bibble, Clod, or Dimple."
Flopwit said, "It was Dimple, Earwig, or me."

Which one spray-painted the principal's Cadillac?

Solution on page 71.

Odd Auditions

Eight actresses attended an audition for a part in Billy Wagjavelin's latest tragedy. After the director saw them all, he listed the auditioners rather cryptically as follows:

1) Eleanor, Ophelia, or Rosaline is second.
2) Adriana or Rosaline is third.
3) Cordelia, Desdemona, or Isabella is fourth.
4) Eleanor, Luciana, or Ophelia is fifth.
5) Adriana, Eleanor, or Luciana is sixth.
6) Isabella or Ophelia is seventh.
7) Adriana or Ophelia is eighth.

Billy's assistant director, Betty, saw the notes and asked him if he had listed the actresses in order of preference. Billy replied that he had not. Can you figure out the method behind the director's notes and determine which actress got the part?

Solution on page 89.

Fine Felines

	Owner's first name	Owner's last name	Cat	Prize
1	Arthur	Brain	KP	potatoes
2	Ben	Doon	Lucy	deodorant
3	Cath	Holick	Minnie	aspirin
4	Des	Parrot	Nellie	sausages
5	Eve	Ninall	Oggy	teabags

In Apple Lane, the results of the Best Cat Competition are about to be announced. However, although each item is in the correct column, only one item in each column is correctly positioned. The following facts are true about the correct order:

1) Ninall is not fourth.
2) Minnie is two places below Cath.
3) Eve is one place below Holick but one above the aspirin.
4) Neither Arthur, KP, nor the deodorant are second.
5) The sausages are two places below Doon but one above Nellie.

Can you find the correct owner's full name, cat, and prize for each position?

Solution on page 85.

See-Saw Sums

Five friends whose weights were in the ratio $1:2:3:4:5$ went to play on a see-saw with two equally spaced seats on each side of the fulcrum. Four climbed on, one to a seat, so that it balanced. Then one got off, and the other three rearranged themselves so the see-saw still balanced. Finally, another climbed off and the remaining two on the see-saw rearranged themselves so they were again balanced. The second one to climb off was lighter than the one who did not participate.

How did the friends balance themselves each time?

Solution on page 88

Careless Whispers

George visited his local swimming pool three times one morning to try to find out what time it closed later that day. On each occasion, two attendants were on duty, and when he asked for the closing time one would whisper information to the other, who would then report that information to George. The trouble was, three attendants worked there, and although two of them always told the truth, the other one always lied. George had no idea who the liar was. A liar would not only whisper the wrong information to the other attendant but would also take whispered information and contradict it. In contrast, a truth-teller would whisper the correct information and faithfully report whispered information whether correct or not. On no two visits did George meet the same combination of two attendants. The possible closing times were on the hour from 1 P.M. to 9 P.M. inclusive, and the information George received about the time was as follows:

1) The hour of the closing time is an even number.
2) The hour of the closing time is not a square number.
3) The hour of the closing time is a prime number.

What was the correct closing time?

Solution on page 86.

Safe Cracker 3

Four different digits from 1 to 9 are required to open a safe.

1) The sum of the first and third digits is less than 9.
2) Exactly one digit is square.
3) The third and fourth digits differ by 3.
4) The first digit is greater than the fourth.
5) The first and second digits add up to 10.

Can you find the four-digit combination?

Solution on page 76.

Counting Sheep 2

9	3	5	3	1	3
2	8	8	5	7	2
1	2	4	7	8	7
8	5	3	2	1	6
1	2	4	6	3	9
9	5	3	4	8	6

Above are 36 pens each containing a number of sheep. A buyer bought all the sheep in 12 of the pens. Delete two numbers from each row and column to leave 24 occupied pens so that each row and column contains 20 sheep.

Solution on page 72.

Logical Line

Three girls (Alice, Barbara, and Connie) and four boys (David, Edward, Frank, and George) arranged themselves in a straight line so that the distribution of boys and girls was symmetrical about the middle person.

1) David stood somewhere to the left of Alice and somewhere to the right of Edward.
2) Frank was somewhere to the left of both Edward and George.
3) Connie was positioned somewhere to the right of George.

What was their order in the line?

Solution on page 79.

Potted Pixies

Four pixies, Flipsy, Gipsy, Hipsy, and Tipsy, lived in four flowerpots A, B, C, and D, at the bottom of the garden, one to a pot. Each pot had a sign on it with a statement about which of the four pixies lived in that particular pot, as follows:

A: "Either Flipsy or Hipsy lives here."
B: "Either Hipsy or Tipsy lives here."
C: "Either Gipsy or Hipsy lives here."
D: "Either Flipsy or Tipsy lives here."

Exactly two statements were true. Gipsy lives next door to Tipsy, but Flipsy is not next door to Hipsy. Can you state the pixie that lives in each flowerpot?

Solution on page 68.

Alien Mutations 3

Above are twelve mutation chambers labeled A to L, surrounded by alien figures. Each alien on the left has passed through the three chambers directly to its right and been transformed into the alien on the far right (e.g., the figure to the left of A has moved through chambers A, B, and C to finish as the one to the right of C). Similarly, each alien shown above the chambers has passed through the four chambers directly below to finish as seen at the bottom. Each chamber always performs a single alteration only (and each chamber must cause a change in both aliens that enter it): specifying head or body shape, adding or removing antennae, adding or removing upper or lower appendages, or specifying posture. What does each chamber do?

Solution on page 76.

23

Eggs Dream Logic Puzzle

At the Sleepwalkers Club annual fair, seven of the members (Alan, Bernie, Cathy, Dave, Ethel, Frank, and George) have just finished competing in the egg-and-spoon race. Despite being incapable of walking in a straight line, they still all managed to finish. The seven members were the only competitors, no two competitors shared a final position, and the following facts are true about their finishing order:

1) Cathy did not finish fourth, fifth, or sixth.
2) The winner was not Alan, Dave, or Frank.
3) Seventh place went to neither Bernie, Cathy, nor Ethel.
4) Third place went to neither Dave, Frank, nor George.
5) Only one of Bernie, Cathy, and Ethel finished in the top three.
6) Alan finished neither second nor third.
7) The fourth-place finisher was neither Alan, Ethel, nor Frank.
8) Bernie was neither fourth nor fifth.

Can you deduce the order in which the seven friends finished?

Solution on page 77.

Custard Close

In a cul-de-sac named Custard Close, there live four men and four women. Whenever one of them gets angry, that person looks for a scapegoat and thrusts a custard pie in the face of a member of the opposite sex living there. That person then does likewise until all eight residents have been pied, so that no person receives more than one pie during the disturbance. On one occasion the following facts applied:

1) Richard pied the woman who pied the man who pied Christine.
2) Stephen pied the woman who pied the man who pied Eleanor.
3) Christine pied the man who pied the woman who pied Quentin.
4) Andrea pied the man who pied the woman who pied Peter.

Who pied Doris?

Solution on page 66.

Safe Cracker 4

Four different digits from 1 to 9 are required to open a safe.

1) The sum of the digits is 20.
2) The first digit is greater than the third.
3) The second and fourth digits differ by at least 5.
4) Exactly two digits are square.
5) The first and fourth digits add up to a prime number.
6) The fourth digit is the lowest.

Can you find the four-digit combination?

Solution on page 78.

Saw Point

In a wood-cutting factory, engineers have newly installed four large sawing machines in an otherwise empty and windowless room. Each machine has an on/off switch attached, and there is no ambiguity as to which switch controls which machine. Outside the door to the room are four safety switches, one for each machine inside. Before reaching the saw, the power for each machine must first pass through the safety switch, and then the machine switch. The problem is, the engineers have not told Dobby the manager how these safety switches match with the machines inside the room.

Later that day, the manager's brother Sparky visits. Dobby takes him inside the room where all four machines are running and explains the problem. The brother announces that he can correctly match the four switches outside the room to the four machines inside, and will only have to leave the room once to do so. The brother works alone, cannot see the machines from outside the room, and solves the problem purely by operating switches. How does he do it?

Solution on page 87.

Citizen's Arrest

	Citizen's first name	Citizen's last name	Culprit's nickname	Culprit's real name
1	Andy	Hook	Slasher	Sid
2	Wes	Ling	Brutal	Baz
3	Joe	Jitsoo	Chopper	Chesney
4	Lesley	Fitt	Desperate	Doug
5	Colin	Daffyds	Razor	Rolf

The prizes are about to be presented for the most courageous citizen's arrest. Listed are the names of both the arresting citizens and the arrested culprits; however, although each item is in the correct column, only one item in each column is correctly positioned. The following facts are true about the correct order:

1) Razor is somewhere above Hook.
2) Baz is one place below Jitsoo but one place above Desperate.
3) Chopper is somewhere below Lesley.
4) Andy is two places above Fitt while Lesley arrested Doug.
5) Chesney is one place below Chopper but one place above Colin.

Can you find the correct arresting citizen's full name and culprit's nickname and real name for each position?

Solution on page 71.

Magic Hats 2

There are six hats: three white and three black. Four friends, Ant, Bendy, Cringe, and Dodgy, are blindfolded and, in turn, a hat is placed on each person's head. The four are then arranged in a circle, the leftover hats are hidden, and the blindfolds removed so that each of the four can see the other three hats but not his own. Each is asked to make a statement about the colors of the three hats he can see. Ant says "two black and one white"; Bendy announces "one black and two white"; Cringe states "at least two black"; and Dodgy says "one black and two white." The white hats are magic; anyone wearing a white one must tell the truth, but anyone wearing a black one may lie or tell the truth. At least one of them is lying.

Can you give the color hat each is wearing and name the liar(s)?

Solution on page 82.

Safe Cracker 5

Four different digits from 1 to 9 are required to open a safe.

1) The third or fourth digit is square but not both.
2) The first and second digits differ by 4.
3) Exactly two digits are prime.
4) The second and fourth digits differ by 2.
5) The sum of the digits is divisible by 7.

Can you find the four-digit combination?

Solution on page 81.

Wed Luck

Four state capitals (Atlanta, Boston, Columbus, and Denver) are the venues for the marriages of four women (Ethel, Freda, Gina, and Harriet), to four men (Ian, Jim, Keith, and Larry). As might be expected, each man marries only one woman in just one location, with no duplications. The relationships are as follows:

1) Ethel does not marry Keith.
2) Atlanta is the venue for either Ian or Larry but not Ethel.
3) Freda marries in either Atlanta or Denver but weds neither Ian nor Larry.
4) Boston is not Larry's venue.
5) Keith goes to neither Boston nor Denver and does not marry Gina.

	Ethel	Freda	Gina	Harriet	Ian	Jim	Keith	Larry
Atlanta								
Boston								
Columbus								
Denver								
Ian				
Jim				
Keith				
Larry				

Can you find the bride and groom for each state capital?

Solution on page 88.

Penalty Shootout

A	B	C
D	E	F

Five soccer players from the Runaround Rovers were ready to take five penalty kicks in a penalty shootout. As shown above, there are six areas of the goal to aim at: A, B, C, D, E, and F. Each penalty kick is aimed at one of the six areas, and on each kick, the goalie dives into one of the six areas to attempt to block it. No two penalty kicks are aimed at the same area, and the goalkeeper does not dive into the same area more than once. If the goalkeeper dives into the same area that the ball is aimed at, then the penalty kick is saved; if not, a goal is scored. Only the second and third penalty kicks are scored.

Here's what we know about the areas the strikers aimed at: Areas B, D, and F were targeted at some point; and area A was targeted sometime after area E. As for the areas the goalkeeper dived into, areas C and D were dived into at some point, area A was sometime before area F, and area B was sometime after area F.

Can you give the five areas that the penalty takers aimed at and the five areas that the goalkeeper dived to?

Solution on page 70.

Alien Mutations 4

Above are twelve mutation chambers labeled A to L, surrounded by alien figures. Each alien on the left has passed through the three chambers directly to its right and been transformed into the alien on the far right (e.g., the figure to the left of A has moved through chambers A, B, and C to finish as the one to the right of C). Similarly, each alien shown above the chambers has passed through the four chambers directly below to finish as seen at the bottom. Each chamber always performs a single alteration only (and each chamber must cause a change in both aliens that enter it): specifying head or body shape, adding or removing antennae, adding or removing upper or lower appendages, or specifying posture. What does each chamber do?

Solution on page 79.

Brain Food

	First name	Last name	Dish
1	Arnie	Grunge	macaroni
2	Barbara	Hobble	lasagna
3	Cathy	Izzy	omelette
4	Dave	Jib	trout
5	Ernie	Krank	salmon
6	Florence	Lisp	risotto

In the village of Dungroovin, the winning entries for the annual Top Chef competition have just been handed in. Although each item is in the correct column, only one item in each column is correctly positioned. Also, we know that:

1) The lasagna is somewhere above Izzy who is somewhere above Ernie.
2) Arnie is two places above Krank who is one place below the risotto.
3) Florence is somewhere above Jib who is somewhere below the macaroni.
4) Jib is two places above the omelette but only one above Barbara.
5) The trout is two places below Grunge and one place above Dave.

Can you find the correct first name, last name, and dish for each position?

Solution on page 91.

Counting Sheep 3

6	8	2	3	3	7
7	1	8	4	5	1
6	7	3	4	2	9
3	9	7	5	1	3
4	1	7	3	6	8
3	2	8	8	9	1

Above are 36 pens each containing a number of sheep. A buyer bought all the sheep in 12 of the pens. Delete two numbers from each row and column to leave 24 occupied pens so that each row and column contains 20 sheep.

Solution on page 86.

Safe Cracker 6

Four different digits from 1 to 9 are required to open a safe.

1) The first digit is greater than the fourth.
2) The sum of the first and third digits is square.
3) The first and second digits differ by 2.
4) The third and fourth digits total 10.

Can you find the four-digit combination?

Solution on page 96.

False Friend

Six friends, Andrea, Brian, Connie, Dan, Elizabeth, and Frank, were interviewed by Officer Whistle about the theft of his hat. One of the six was a habitual liar, and this was the person who had stolen it. The other five knew who had done it and always told the truth.

In turn, each of the six was asked to name three suspects for the theft. This person then whispered a response to another of the six who then reported it to Officer Whistle. A truth teller always included the culprit in his or her three suspects and also accurately reported the whispered three suspects. The liar did not include himself in his three suspects and when given another's response, reported the other three suspects to the officer.

1) Dan reported that Andrea had said "Andrea, Connie, or Elizabeth."
2) Connie reported that Elizabeth had said "Brian, Dan, or Elizabeth."
3) Frank reported that Brian had said "Connie, Dan, or Frank."
4) Elizabeth reported that Dan had said "Brian, Connie, or Elizabeth."
5) Andrea reported that Frank had said "Brian, Dan, or Elizabeth."
6) Brian reported that Connie had said "Connie, Dan, or Frank."

Can you discover who stole Officer Whistle's hat?

Solution on page 83.

Boxing Clever

	Nickname	Real name	Knockout punch	Winning round
1	Iron	Mike	hook	3
2	Basher	Bloggs	uppercut	4
3	Lightning	Sid	left jab	7
4	Sugar	Roy	body shot	5
5	Hitman	Henry	right jab	1
6	Killer	Joe	straight	8

The results of the International Boxing Championship are ready to be announced. However, although each item is in the correct column, only one item in each column is correctly positioned. The following facts are true about the correct order:

1) Sugar is one place above Joe.
2) Round 4 is one place below Bloggs but one above Lightning.
3) The body shot is two places below Basher but three below Sid.
4) Basher is not adjacent to Hitman.
5) The left jab is one place below round 1.
6) Hitman is one place above round 8 but two below the hook.
7) Mike is one place above round 5 but three above the right jab.

Can you give the correct name, knockout punch, and winning round for each boxer?

Solution on page 72.

Cinema Seats

Sixteen friends went to the movies and chose a 4×4 square of seats according to the following plan. (Note that "to the left" and "to the right" do not necessarily imply "in the same row," and "above" and "below" do not necessarily imply "in the same column.")

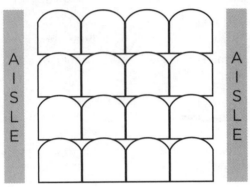

1) George is one column to the right of Elsie.
2) Ian is three columns to the left of Nora who is one row above Colin.
3) Amy is one row below Bernard who is two columns to the left of Elsie.
4) Julie, who is not in an aisle seat, is one column to the left of Keith and one row above Oliver.
5) Frank is two rows below Amy who is one column to the right of Frank.
6) Minnie is three rows above Oliver, who is both one column to the right of Julie and not in an aisle seat.
7) George is one row above Ian; neither is in the front or back row of the 4×4 square.
8) Linda is one column to the left of Minnie who is two columns to the left of Penny.
9) Colin is three rows below Harry and Dave is two columns to the right of Amy.
10) Elsie is two rows above Penny.

Can you identify the occupant of each seat?

Solution on page 65.

Space Race

Four intergalactic space beings (Bleep, Digit, Ping, and Zap), from the planets Appa, Blob, Moot, and Pag, decide to have a competition to see which of their space vehicles (each fueled either by diesel, fission, hydrogen, or paraffin), can travel the quickest. Each being originates from one planet only and uses one type of fuel only, with no duplications. The following facts are known:

1) The hydrogen-powered vehicle's pilot, who is not from Pag, is either Ping or Zap.
2) Ping's vehicle is fueled by neither diesel nor paraffin.
3) Blob is not the birthplace of Digit or Zap.
4) The paraffin-powered vehicle is from either Blob or Moot but is not piloted by Digit.
5) Zap, who is not from Moot, has a vehicle powered by either hydrogen or paraffin.
6) Diesel does not power the vehicle from Moot.
7) The fission-powered vehicle is not Bleep's and neither is it from Blob.

	Appa	Blob	Moot	Pag	diesel	fission	hydrogen	paraffin
Bleep								
Digit								
Ping								
Zap								
diesel				
fission				
hydrogen				
paraffin				

Can you find the name, home planet, and vehicle fuel for each pilot?

Solution on page 67.

Alien Mutations 5

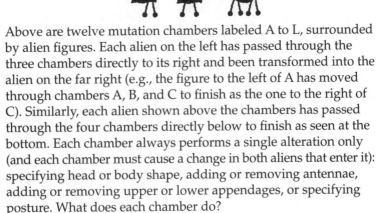

Above are twelve mutation chambers labeled A to L, surrounded by alien figures. Each alien on the left has passed through the three chambers directly to its right and been transformed into the alien on the far right (e.g., the figure to the left of A has moved through chambers A, B, and C to finish as the one to the right of C). Similarly, each alien shown above the chambers has passed through the four chambers directly below to finish as seen at the bottom. Each chamber always performs a single alteration only (and each chamber must cause a change in both aliens that enter it): specifying head or body shape, adding or removing antennae, adding or removing upper or lower appendages, or specifying posture. What does each chamber do?

Solution on page 83.

Time and Temperature

Professor Neuron has been observing the sunset, and on each day of one particular week he recorded the temperature outside his house at the precise moment he saw the sun disappear. This has given him a different temperature reading for each of the seven days. To organize his list, Professor Neuron has written down the days in descending order by temperature; that is, the day with the highest temperature is first on the list, and the day with the lowest temperature is last. His list has the following features:

1) Wednesday is less than five places from Thursday.
2) Saturday is two places from Monday.
3) Friday is next to Sunday.
4) Thursday is at most two places from Tuesday.
5) Tuesday is at least five places from Monday.
6) Wednesday is below Sunday, but less than three places away.

Once you've determined the order of days, you can use these details to determine the recorded temperature for each day:

1) One day's temperature was equal to the product of the number of letters in the list's previous day and the number of letters in the list's subsequent day.
2) One day's temperature was equal to three times the sum of the number of letters in the list's previous day and the number of letters in the list's subsequent day.
3) One day's temperature was equal to the sum of the number of letters in all the previous days on the list plus 25.
4) One of the two highest temperatures was the product of the four digits in the two lowest temperatures.
5) No two adjacent temperatures on the list had a difference greater than 12 or smaller than 2.

Can you discover Professor Neuron's complete list in descending order of recorded temperature?

Solution on page 74.

Apart Meant

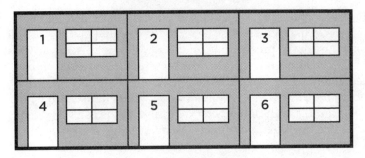

A police officer was carrying out an investigation at the six apartments at Hope House. Each apartment had a single occupant whose name the officer hoped to discover: three men (Bob, Dave, and Jim) and three women (Amy, Sally, and Tina). However, knowing that the officer's visit was impending, none of the tenants answered the door when he knocked, although each had left a (truthful) note pinned to his or her front door. For the three upper floor apartments, in no particular order, the notes were as follows.

a) Bob is in the apartment directly below me.
b) Amy is in an apartment next to this one.
c) Jim lives here.

For the three ground floor apartments, again in no particular order, the notes were as follows.

d) Either Dave or Jim lives in the apartment directly above me.
e) As you face my door, Tina's apartment is to your left on this floor.
f) Sally lives here.

Just as the police officer had finished reading the notes he saw a female resident peep through the curtains at apartment #5.

Can you match the names to each apartment number?

Solution on page 77.

Mad Movies

	First name	Last name	Movie	Director
1	Alf	Grump	*Ben-Him*	Spoolbag
2	Bert	Howdydo	*Cyclo*	Tapintoono
3	Connie	Ink	*Eight*	Hitchfrock
4	Doris	Jiff	*Low Midnight*	Vastcounti
5	Edgar	Klink	*Queen Kang*	Loser
6	Fred	Limpet	*Rebuke Her*	Einstein

Mad Movies magazine has printed its list of the top six film performances of all time. Although each item is in the correct column, only one entry in each column is correctly positioned. The following facts are true about the correct order:

1) Alf is neither Klink nor Howdydo.
2) Tapintoono is two above *Ben-Him*.
3) Doris is two below *Eight* but one below Vastcounti.
4) Hitchfrock is one above *Rebuke Her* but two below Howdydo.
5) Grump is two above Einstein but one above Edgar, whose position is not adjacent to Doris's.
6) Jiff is one below *Cyclo* and one above Fred.

Can you find the correct actor's name, film, and director for each position?

Solution on page 92.

Pies and Lies

Four siblings, Casey, Macey, Stacey, and Tracy, had just raided the kitchen windowsill for Mama Pip's hot apple pies (she had left them there to cool), but only two ate any. When Mama Pip noticed some of her pies missing, she questioned the children in pairs to try to get the culprits to confess.

Two of the four were habitual helpers and the other two were reliable rebels. Each pair questioned gave Mama Pip two names: either the innocent two or the guilty two. One of the questioned pair would whisper two names to the other: the correct two if a helper, and the incorrect two if a rebel. The other would then report this to Mama Pip, exactly repeating it if a helper, or changing the names to the other two if a rebel.

The four pairs questioned were Casey and Tracey, Macey and Stacey, Macey and Tracey, and Stacey and Tracey. However, Mama Pip had been peeping through the kitchen window, saw who the two culprits were, and knew that exactly two of the four statements were incorrect. In the four pairs given above, one of the rebels has appeared with both helpers.

If the two rebels were guilty, who ate the pies?

Solution on page 73.

Doing Time

	Nickname	Real name	Former occupation	Crime
1	Awful	Mike	tailor	burglary
2	Bonkers	Norman	salesman	con game
3	Crazy	Oliver	welder	pickpocketing
4	Desperate	Paul	electrician	shoplifting
5	Egghead	Quentin	judge	fraud
6	Fingers	Ronnie	dentist	bigamy

At Penance Prison, a list of the longest serving inmates has been posted on the notice board. However, the notice has been defaced and although each item is in the correct column, only one entry in each column is correctly positioned. The following facts are true about the correct order:

1) The judge is one row below Quentin, whose nickname is Bonkers.
2) The salesman is somewhere above the dentist and two places above the pickpocket.
3) Egghead is two places below Norman.
4) Mike is three places above the bigamist.
5) Fingers is immediately below Egghead but three places below the tailor.
6) Bonkers is one row below the fraudster and somewhere above Crazy.
7) The con man is two rows above Oliver.

Can you find the correct name, former occupation, and crime for each position?

Solution on page 66.

Counting Sheep 4

4	8	3	8	1	7
4	1	6	4	9	2
2	8	6	3	3	9
5	9	3	5	9	3
5	3	5	3	7	4
9	2	6	8	2	1

Above are 36 pens each containing a number of sheep. A buyer bought all the sheep in 12 of the pens. Delete two numbers from each row and column to leave 24 occupied pens so that each row and column contains 20 sheep.

Solution on page 91.

Safe Cracker 7

Four different digits from 1 to 9 are required to open a safe.

1) The second and third digits differ by 2.
2) The fourth digit is greater than the second.
3) The sum of the third and fourth digits is less than 7.
4) Exactly two digits are prime.
5) The first and third digits total 12.

Can you find the four-digit combination?

Solution on page 86.

Alien Mutations 6

Above are twelve mutation chambers labeled A to L, surrounded by alien figures. Each alien on the left has passed through the three chambers directly to its right and been transformed into the alien on the far right (e.g., the figure to the left of A has moved through chambers A, B, and C to finish as the one to the right of C). Similarly, each alien shown above the chambers has passed through the four chambers directly below to finish as seen at the bottom. Each chamber always performs a single alteration only (and each chamber must cause a change in both aliens that enter it): specifying head or body shape, adding or removing antennae, adding or removing upper or lower appendages, or specifying posture. What does each chamber do?

Solution on page 84.

45

Crime Wave

	Title	Last name	Location	Weapon
1	Professor	Carrot	shed	blowtorch
2	Duchess	Indigo	greenhouse	dynamite
3	Earl	Grey	attic	acid
4	Lord	Tomato	basement	poker
5	Doctor	Blew	bathroom	cyanide
6	Sir	Mauve	playroom	hammer

Inspector Twiggit has just announced his top six suspects for the murder of Lady Limpwit, who had earlier been found floating in the pool at Muckrake Mansions. Unfortunately, his assistant has written them down incorrectly. Although each item is in the correct column, only one entry in each column is correctly positioned. The following facts are true about the correct order:

1) The blowtorch is somewhere above the greenhouse and the duchess.
2) The earl is two above Tomato.
3) The acid is one place below the shed and one above Mauve.
4) The professor is three above the bathroom.
5) Grey is three below the dynamite.
6) The playroom is one place below the poker but two below the lord.
7) Neither the professor nor the earl is suspected of using the poker.
8) Indigo is somewhere above Carrot.

Can you find the correct name, location, and weapon for each position?

Solution on page 75.

Ranking Officers

Six officers in the U.S. army were waiting for four jeeps to arrive. Their ranks in descending order were general, colonel, major, captain, sergeant, and corporal. When the jeeps pulled up, only four of the six climbed in, one to a jeep. Numbering the jeeps 1 to 4 corresponding to their order of arrival, the following facts are true about who used them:

1) Jeep 2 was taken by a higher-ranking officer than the officer in jeep 3.
2) The officer who took jeep 1 was two positions away in the given order of ranks from the officer who took jeep 3.
3) The captain and the sergeant were not in consecutive jeeps.
4) Jeep 4 was taken by an officer three positions away in the given order of ranks from the one who took jeep 2.
5) The officer who took jeep 1 had a lower rank than the one in jeep 4.

Can you find the officer who took each jeep?

Solution on page 83.

Safe Cracker 8

Four different digits from 1 to 9 are required to open a safe.

1) Exactly two digits are prime.
2) The sum of the first and third digits is even.
3) The first and fourth digits differ by 2.
4) The third digit is at least three times the second.
5) The sum of the third and fourth digits is at least 15.

Can you find the four-digit combination?

Solution on page 89.

Corridor Conundrum

An ancient explorer enters a magical corridor where he passes through four doors (A, B, C, and D) into a room with three more doors (1, 2, and 3). One of the three numbered doors leads to eternal happiness while the other two lead to unending misery. The doors A, B, C, and D are each attended by a guard, exactly one of whom always tells the truth; the other three always lie. As the pleasure-seeker passes through each of the four lettered doors, he asks that door's guard which of the three numbered doors leads to eternal happiness, and he receives one of the three numbers as a response. As for the room at the end of the corridor, there is also a guard on each of the doors 1, 2, and 3. One guard always tells the truth while the other two always lie.

Before entering the corridor, the explorer has no information as to which two of the seven guards are the truth-tellers, but he does know that the door that leads to eternal happiness is guarded by a truth-teller. Furthermore, when he gets into the room he must point to one of the doors and ask only one of the three guards the following question "Does this door lead to eternal happiness?" He must then choose the correct door from the "yes" or "no" the guard gives in response. How can the pleasure-seeker be sure which door leads to eternal happiness?

Solution on page 84.

Pets Around the World

Five people (Arthur, Benny, Cathy, Doris, and Eve) own five pets (a cat, a dog, an elephant, a frog, and a goat) in five cities (Berlin, Helsinki, London, New York, and Paris). Each owner has only one pet in just one location. The relationships are as follows:

1) The New York owner is either Benny, Cathy, or Eve, but the pet there is neither an elephant nor a goat.
2) The frog owner is neither Cathy nor Eve.
3) Benny owns either a cat, elephant, or goat, but not in Berlin.
4) The owner of the elephant is in neither London nor Paris and is not Arthur.
5) The Helsinki owner is either Arthur, Benny, or Eve.
6) Arthur does not live in Paris.
7) The cat owner lives in neither Berlin nor New York and is not Doris.
8) Cathy owns neither the cat nor the dog and lives in neither Berlin nor Paris.

Can you find the owner's name and pet for each location?

	cat	dog	elephant	frog	goat	Berlin	Helsinki	London	New York	Paris
Arthur										
Benny										
Cathy										
Doris										
Eve										
Berlin					
Helsinki					
London					
New York					
Paris					

Solution on page 80.

Alien Mutations 7

Above are sixteen mutation chambers labeled A to P, surrounded by alien figures. Each alien on the left has passed through the four chambers directly to its right and been transformed into the alien on the far right (e.g., the figure to the left of A has moved through chambers A, B, C, and D to finish as the one to the right of D). Similarly, each alien shown above the chambers has passed through the four chambers directly below to finish as seen at the bottom. Each chamber always performs a single alteration only (and each chamber must cause a change in both aliens that enter it): specifying head or body shape, adding or removing antennae, adding or removing upper or lower appendages, or specifying posture. What does each chamber do?

Solution on page 86.

Talent Ted

	First name	Last name	Act	Items used
1	Fred	Bloggs	spinning	plates
2	Peter	Hout	throwing	knives
3	Dee	Looded	waving	flowers
4	Alf	Arted	juggling	carrots
5	Joe	King	eating	eggs
6	Carol	Singer	smashing	bottles

Ted Sparkle, one of the judges of *America's Hot Talent*, has compiled a list of his top six acts. Although each item is in the correct column, he has only correctly positioned one item in each column, because ... well, he just has. The following facts are certain about the correct order:

1) The plates are two places above Singer.
2) Looded is one place below waving, which is two places below Dee.
3) Alf is one place from Arted.
4) The flowers are somewhere above juggling, which is somewhere above Hout.
5) Fred is three places above eating, which is two below the carrots.
6) Spinning is one place below Carol, who is one below the bottles.

Can you give the correct full name of the performer and the act description for each position?

Solution on page 78.

The Singing Citizen

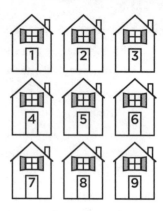

Three criminals and six honest citizens live in a 3×3 block of nine houses arranged as shown above, one to each house. No criminal shares a row or column with another criminal, and a criminal always tells lies while an honest citizen always tells the truth.

The police received a complaint that one of the six honest citizens was keeping the neighborhood awake every night by singing opera loudly, so they interviewed each occupant about the singing citizen's house number. The nine interviewees (each of whom knows which house contains the singer) gave a list of house numbers as follows, claiming the culprit lived in one of them.

Interviewee	Claim
1	3, 4, 6, 7, 8, 9
2	1, 2, 3, 5, 7, 9
3	1, 2, 4, 5, 6, 8
4	1, 2, 5, 6, 7, 9
5	1, 3, 4, 6, 7, 8
6	2, 3, 4, 5, 8, 9
7	1, 2, 3, 4, 8, 9
8	4, 5, 6, 7, 8, 9
9	1, 2, 3, 5, 6, 7

Can you determine which house the singing citizen lives in?

Solution on page 82.

Gone Away

	First name	Last name	Destination	Days
1	Arthur	Rich	Barcelona	4
2	Barbara	Drip	Rome	5
3	Connie	Castaway	Corfu	7
4	Dave	Monk	Ibiza	10
5	Ethel	Wise	Minorca	12
6	Freddie	Idle	Tenerife	14

Hopeful Holidays magazine has just published its top six holiday destinations together with the name of the reviewers who chose each of them, and how many days they spent on their trips. However, the copy editor's concentration seems to have left him. Although each item in its correct column, only one item in each column is correctly positioned. The following facts are true about the correct order:

1) The 12-day holiday is one place above Freddie.
2) Corfu is three places above Drip.
3) Wise is two places below Connie and one above the 4-day holiday.
4) The 7-day holiday is one place above Barcelona and three above Barbara.
5) The 10-day holiday is three places below Monk and two below Tenerife.
6) Idle is two places above Arthur and one below Rome.

Can you find the correct reviewer's name, destination, and length of stay for each position?

Solution on page 81.

Alien Mutations 8

Above are sixteen mutation chambers labeled A to P, surrounded by alien figures. Each alien on the left has passed through the four chambers directly to its right and been transformed into the alien on the far right (e.g., the figure to the left of A has moved through chambers A, B, C, and D to finish as the one to the right of D). Similarly, each alien shown above the chambers has passed through the four chambers directly below to finish as seen at the bottom. Each chamber always performs a single alteration only (and each chamber must cause a change in both aliens that enter it): specifying head or body shape, adding or removing antennae, adding or removing upper or lower appendages, or specifying posture. What does each chamber do?

Solution on page 92.

54

Wrong Feat

	Husband	Wife	Dance	Costume color
1	Barney	Betty	cha-cha	blue
2	Fred	Wilma	fandango	green
3	Gavin	Stacey	jive	orange
4	Terry	June	paso doble	purple
5	Mork	Mindy	salsa	turquoise
6	Will	Grace	tango	yellow

At the Couples' Comedy Dance Championships the judges have decided on their top six couples. However, the results have been incorrectly copied, and although each item is in the correct column, only one entry in each column is correctly positioned. The following facts are true about the correct order:

1) The salsa is somewhere above Mork.
2) The tango is one place above Wilma and two above Gavin.
3) Betty is somewhere below the green costumes.
4) The orange costumes are not next to the yellow ones.
5) Terry is one place below the fandango and one above the yellow costumes.
6) The orange costumes are two places above the paso doble and one below Stacey.
7) The turquoise costumes are one place below Will and one above June.

Can you find the correct husband, wife, dance, and costume color for each position?

Solution on page 69.

Safe Cracker 9

Four different digits from 1 to 9 are required to open a safe.

1) The fourth digit is greater than the second.
2) The sum of the second and third digits is 11.
3) Neither the third nor fourth digit is square.
4) The first digit is greater than the third.
5) The first and fourth digits total 13.

Can you find the four-digit combination?

Solution on page 71.

Key Caper

Alan, Ben, Carrie, Danae, Ella, and Francis were caught trying to break into their classroom, which was always locked during lunch hour. They had managed to obtain a spare key, and just as they were about to open the classroom door, the principal turned up unexpectedly. The students nervously passed it around from one to the other in a repeating sequence of six, no student appearing twice in that sequence. When questioned by the principal, each student named several others that he or she might have passed it on to, one of which was correct in each case, as follows.

Alan → Carrie or Danae or Francis
Ben → Ella or Francis
Carrie → Alan or Ben or Danae
Danae → Ben or Ella or Francis
Ella → Ben or Carrie
Francis → Alan or Ben or Ella

In the first pass of the sequence, Francis received the key sometime after Alan had it. Alan was not one of the first two in the sequence of six to hold the key, and Ben was not one of the last two to hold it. In what order was the key passed around?

Solution on page 85.

Medic Hate

	Patient's first name	Patient's last name	Ailment	Remedy
1	Andy	Grumble	laryngitis	leeches
2	Beryl	Shirker	nosebleed	snake blood
3	Connie	Worrie	influenza	eye of newt
4	Daniel	Jape	measles	frog tears
5	Edward	Complane	gout	cold bath
6	Fay	Pawlea	heartburn	bloodletting

The Muddletown Medical Council have compiled a list of the most disturbing complaints received about inappropriate remedies prescribed by doctors. Although the researcher has placed each item in the correct column, only one item in each column is correctly positioned. The following facts are true about the correct order:

1) The nosebleed is not adjacent to laryngitis.
2) Andy, Jape, and the leeches are somewhere above the measles.
3) Laryngitis is one place above Connie, who is one place above the frog tears.
4) Complane is one place below Edward and two places above the eye of newt.
5) Beryl is not adjacent to Connie.
6) The cold bath is two places above Grumble and one above gout.
7) Beryl is one below Pawlea and one above the nosebleed.

Can you give the correct patients' names, ailments, and prescribed remedies for each position?

Solution on page 93.

Counting Sheep 5

3	4	6	7	4	1
3	7	3	2	7	8
4	1	7	8	7	1
5	4	4	3	2	9
6	8	2	3	7	3
8	1	9	1	4	2

Above are 36 pens each containing a number of sheep. A buyer bought all the sheep in 12 of the pens. Delete two numbers from each row and column to leave 24 occupied pens so that each row and column contains 20 sheep.

Solution on page 96.

Safe Cracker 10

Four different digits from 1 to 9 are required to open a safe.

1) The sum of the first and fourth digits is a square.
2) The second and third digits differ by 1.
3) Either the first or second digit is square, but not both.
4) The first digit is bigger than the third.
5) The sum of the third and fourth digits is greater than 13.

Can you find the four-digit combination?

Solution on page 84.

Terrible Tunes

Five friends (Bob, Cindy, Delilah, Evan, and Felicity) with more free time than talent decide to form a band. Each plays one instrument (bass, drums, guitar, piano, or trumpet) and suggests one band name (the Drips, Folly, the Goons, Humbug, and the Muddles). The following facts are known:

1) Evan plays guitar or trumpet but didn't suggest the Drips or the Goons.
2) The Muddles was suggested by either Delilah or Evan, but not by the guitarist or the trumpeter.
3) Cindy suggested neither Folly nor Humbug, and does not play the drums.
4) The Drips was suggested by either the bassist, drummer, or guitarist, but not by Bob.
5) The drummer suggested either the Drips or the Muddles.
6) The Goons wasn't suggested by Felicity, nor was it suggested by the pianist.
7) Felicity is either the guitarist or trumpeter.
8) Humbug wasn't the guitarist's or pianist's suggestion.

Can you determine who played (and suggested) what?

Solution on page 90.

Holmes's Sweet Home

Sherlock Holmes was reading quietly one evening when a football shattered his living room window. Holmes leapt to his feet and spotted Professor Moriarty's six children (Abraham, Benjamin, Catherine, Daniel, Elizabeth, and Florence) outside his house. Throwing down his "Teach Yourself Logic" book, he rushed into the street and apprehended three of the children as the rest ran away.

Knowing that the children were bright, Holmes decided to ask each of the three a question to find out who had broken the window. He knew that each child either consistently told lies or consistently told the truth, but did not know who told what.

Catherine was asked: "Is it true that exactly one of the following statements is true: 'One of Abraham, Benjamin, Elizabeth, and Florence broke the window' and 'You tell the truth'?"

Daniel was asked: "Is it true that exactly one of the following statements is true: 'Precisely two of Benjamin, Catherine, and yourself didn't break the window' and 'You tell lies'?"

Florence was asked: "Is it true that the following statements are either both true or both false: 'One of the other two present broke the window' and 'You tell the truth'?"

Each answered either "yes" or "no," and one of the three answers differed from the other two.

Which child broke the window?

Solution on page 76.

The Burgling Brothers

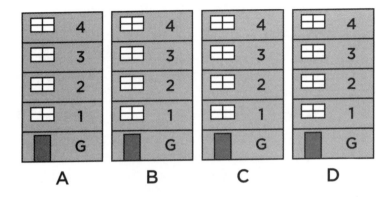

One night, four burgling brothers visited four apartment buildings, A, B, C, and D, one burglar per building. Each building has four apartments numbered from 1 to 4, one on each floor, each of which can be reached only by elevator. In any building, all apartments are to be visited once only. All four burglars enter a building on the ground floor G and travel by elevator to reach the door of their first choices of apartment simultaneously. They also reach the doors of their second, third, and fourth choices at the same time. However, at no time are any two brothers burgling on the same floor.

1) After burgling the first apartment, only the burglars in buildings A and C went up in the elevator to reach their second apartment. The other two went down.
2) After burgling the second apartment, only those in B and C took the elevator up to reach their third apartment. The other two went down. Each of the four, however, traveled to a floor adjacent to the one he had just left on that trip.
3) After burgling the third apartment, no burglar went to an adjacent floor to reach his fourth apartment.

Can you give the order in which the burgling brothers visited the four apartments in each of the buildings A, B, C, and D?

Solution on page 64.

Gift Gaffes

	Recipient	Hotel	Color of wrapping	Gift
1	Aaron	Biltless	blue	book
2	Billy	Five Seasons	green	computer
3	Cher	Marrioff	orange	DVD
4	Des	Nights Inn	red	guitar
5	Eva	Singletree	silver	phone
6	Fiona	Ritzy	turquoise	TV
7	George	Weighaton	yellow	violin

Santa has compiled a list of deliveries to children vacationing with their families in Grateful Grove, so he'll remember to deliver gifts to their hotels rather than their homes. However, he became inattentive after one too many sugar plums, and although each item is in the correct column, only one entry in each column is correctly positioned. The following facts are true about the correct order:

1) The green wrapping paper is one below Aaron and two above the Ritzy.
2) The Marrioff is somewhere above Cher.
3) The computer is not above the blue wrapping paper.
4) The turquoise wrapping paper is one above the TV, which is two above the phone.
5) George is two below the Singletree and two above the book.
6) The Nights Inn is three above Des, who is two below the silver wrapping paper and three below the guitar.
7) Fiona is one below the orange wrapping paper and one above the Weighaton.

Can you find the correct recipient, hotel, wrapping paper color, and gift for each position?

Solution on pages 94–95.

Answers

7 Safe Cracker 1

The combination is 1263.

61 The Burgling Brothers

The orders are A: 2431, B: 3124, C: 1342, and D: 4213.

Whoever burgled the fourth floor second must have gone up before the second burglary and down after. The only building where this happened was A. Since the second and third burglaries were on adjacent floors (per clue 2), the A burglar went to 3 third, and since the third and fourth were not consecutive (per clue 3), the A burglaries in order were 2431.

Similarly, whoever burgled the first floor second must have gone down before the second burglary and up after. The only building where this happened was B. Since the second and third burglaries were on adjacent floors, the B burglar went to 2 third, and since the third and fourth were not consecutive, the B burglaries in order were 3124.

Since those two burglars both went to 2 and 3 first and third and no burglars were ever on the same floor at the same time, the C burglar went to 1 and 4 first and third. Since he went up twice to get from his first burglary to his third, he went to 1 first and 4 third, and since his second and third burglaries were on adjacent floors, his burglaries in order were 1342, leaving 4213 for building D.

9 Alien Mutations 1

A: head becomes square; B: add antennae; C: add lower appendages ("lower" meaning further from the neck); D: body becomes square; E: posture becomes upright; F: remove upper appendages; G: remove lower appendages; H: body becomes circular; I: posture becomes horizontal.

13 Counting Sheep 1

	7	9		1	3
8	3		5	4	
	8	2	9		1
8	2	1		9	
1		8	4		7
3			2	6	9

Many approaches to the solution are possible, but one option is to start with row 4, which starts out totaling 27. The only digits in that row that add up to 7 are the 3 and 4. That leaves 26 in column 4 and 24 in column 6, so we delete the 6 and 4 in those columns, respectively. Row 2 now adds up to 21, so delete the 1, which leaves 25 in column 3. Delete the 5, leaving 24 in row 6. After deleting the 4, we have a total of 25 in column 2, so delete that column's 5, leaving 23 in row 5. After deleting that row's 3, column 5 totals 26, but we can't delete the 6 in the bottom row (which already has two deleted numbers), so delete the one in row 3. In column 1, delete the digits in rows 1 and 3 (the only rows with only one deleted digit) to complete the puzzle.

16 Safe Cracker 2

The combination is 9675.

36 Cinema Seats

Row A, left to right: Bernard, Minnie, Harry, Dave; row B, left to right: Linda, Amy, Elsie, George; row C, left to right: Ian, Julie, Keith, Nora; row D, left to right: Frank, Colin, Oliver, Penny. The best approach to the solution is to consider the row and column information separately, and write the deduced positions to the left of each row and above each column. Then deductions can be made by seeing which letters share a row and column.

25 Custard Close

From conditions (1) and (4), there are two possible lines:
A→R→woman→P→C, and R→A→man→C→P. (The two
sequences in those clues must overlap; otherwise the sequence
would contain two women in a row or two men in a row.)
With condition (2) these become S→A→R→E→P→C and
R→A→S→C→P→E. Finally, (3) only fits with the second of those
possibilities—the first causes there to be more links in the chain
than there are residents—giving us R→A→S→C→P→E→Q. So
Doris can only fit between Q and R, and Quentin pied Doris.

43 Doing Time

	Nickname	Name	Occupation	Crime
1	Awful	Norman	tailor	shoplifting
2	Desperate	Mike	welder	con game
3	Egghead	Ronnie	electrician	burglary
4	Fingers	Oliver	salesman	fraud
5	Bonkers	Quentin	dentist	bigamy
6	Crazy	Paul	judge	pickpocketing

From (5), Egghead and Fingers can't both be correct in 5 and
6, so they're either in 3 and 4 or 4 and 5 respectively, with the
tailor in 1 or 2 and, from (3), Norman also in 1 or 2. From (4),
Mike can't be in 1 or Mike and Norman would both be correct
in 1 and 2, so Mike is in either 2 or 3 with the bigamist in 5 or
6. All those items are fixed relative to each other, so Norman,
Mike, Egghead, and Fingers are in a block of four consecutive
positions, either 1–4 or 2–5. From (1), Bonkers and Quentin are
in the same position, so they must be in one of the positions not
occupied by Norman, Mike, Egghead, and Fingers. From (1),
Bonkers and Quentin are one above the judge and, from (6) one
below the fraudster, so they cannot be in 1 or 6 and must be in
5 (where Quentin is correct), and now all the items from (1), (3),
(4), (5), and (6) can be placed; of those items, the tailor is correct
in 1. From (2), the salesman must be in 4 and the pickpocket in
6, which leaves 5 as the only available position for the dentist
below the salesman. From (7), Oliver can't also be correct in 3, so
he's in 4 with the con man correct in 2. Awful must be the correct
nickname in 1; everything else can be placed by elimination.

16 Right on Queue

The order from first to last is Fred, Barbara, Colin, Doris, Andy, Ethel. From (4), the pair in second and third place and the pair in fifth and sixth place must either be AE and BC in some order, each pair having a total of $14, or they are BF and CE in some order, each pair having a total of $20. D is in neither of those sets, so D is either first or fourth in line. From (2), the pair in third and fourth can only be AD or CD in some order. However, we have seen that D is not third in line, so D is fourth and either A or C is third. This leaves the possibilities (a) FEADBC, (b) FEADCB, (c) FBCDAE, (d) FBCDEA, (e) AECDBF, or (f) AECDFB. From (1), we can have (a), (c), (d), or (e); condition (3) reduces these to (c) only.

37 Space Race

Bleep is from Blob and uses paraffin; Digit is from Pag and uses diesel; Ping is from Moot and uses fission; and Zap is from Appa and uses hydrogen. From the given clues, the following table can be constructed where ×'s indicate eliminated possibilities:

	Appa	Blob	Moot	Pag	diesel	fission	hydrogen	paraffin
Bleep						×	×	
Digit	×						×	×
Ping					×			×
Zap	×	×			×	×		
diesel			×					
fission		×						
hydrogen				×				
paraffin	×			×				

Although no row or column gives enough information to solidly identify any pairings right away, note that Zap comes from either Appa or Pag and pilots either the hydrogen or paraffin vehicle, but that the paraffin vehicle's pilot comes from either Blob or Moot, so Zap must pilot the hydrogen-powered vehicle. Everything else follows by elimination.

10 Magic Hats 1

Ant is wearing a white hat, Bendy is lying and wears a black hat, and Cringe wears a black hat. Remember that while a liar always has a black hat, a truth-teller *might* have a black hat. Anyone wearing a white hat must be a truth-teller, but a black hat wearer can be either a truth-teller or a liar.

Bendy must be wearing a black hat, because either he's telling the truth and sees two white hats (in which case there are no white hats remaining for him to wear), or he's lying, in which case his hat must be black. Ant's statement, therefore, is true (though his hat may be either color). If Cringe is lying about seeing only one black hat, then he must be seeing two—but then there is no third hat that he, as a liar, can be wearing. Therefore, his statement is true, and Ant's hat is white. Since Ant and Cringe are telling the truth, Bendy's statement must be the lie, and he does not see two white hats, so Cringe's hat must be black.

22 Potted Pixies

Hipsy lived in pot A, Gipsy in B, Tipsy in C, and Flipsy in D. There are only six possible arrangements of two true (T) and two false (F) statements among the pots' signs; the consequences of each arrangement are shown in the table below. The bottom row indicates whether or not it is possible to account for all four pixies in that column.

	1	2	3	4	5	6
pot A	T: FH	T: FH	T: FH	F: GT	F: GT	F: GT
pot B	T: HT	F: FG	F: FG	T: HT	T: HT	F: FG
pot C	F: FT	T: GH	F: FT	T: GH	F: FT	T: GH
pot D	F: GH	F: GH	T: FT	F: GH	T: FT	T: FT
	yes	no	yes	no	yes	yes

From (1), the options are HTFG, FHTG; from (3), HGFT, HGTF; from (5), GHFT, GHTF; and from (6), GFHT, TGHF. Since G must be next to T, we can narrow the options down to FHTG, HGTF, or TGHF. The added condition that F is not next to H gives HGTF as the only possibility.

55 Wrong Feat

	Husband	Wife	Dance	Costume
1	Will	Mindy	cha-cha	green
2	Barney	Stacey	salsa	turquoise
3	Mork	June	fandango	orange
4	Terry	Betty	tango	blue
5	Fred	Wilma	paso doble	yellow
6	Gavin	Grace	jive	purple

From (6), orange is in 2, 3, or 4. From (5), yellow is in 3, 4, 5, or 6, but if yellow were in 3, orange would be adjacent to it in 2 or 4, which contradicts (4), so that's not the case. If yellow were in 4 with the fandango correct in 2, orange would have to be in 2 with the paso doble also correct in 4, so yellow isn't in 4 either. From (7), turquoise is in 2, 3, 4, or 5, but if it were correct in 5, yellow would have to be also correct in 6, so turquoise isn't in 5. From (6), if Stacey were correct in 3 with orange in 4, June couldn't also be correct in 4, so, from (7), June would be in 5, but then turquoise would also have to be in 4, so Stacey isn't in 3. From (2), if Wilma were correct in 2, Gavin would be correct in 3. Then Stacey would be in 1, paso doble in 4, fandango in 3, and Terry also correct in 4, a contradiction, so Wilma isn't in 2. If Wilma were in 3 with Gavin in 4, Terry would be in 5, yellow correct in 6, and the fandango in 4, which would force the paso doble to be in 5 with orange also correct in 3, also impossible, so Wilma isn't in 3. If Wilma were in 4 with Gavin in 5 and tango in 3, then Terry would be in 4 with fandango also in 3, yet another contradiction, so Wilma isn't in 4 either and must be in 5 with Gavin in 6 and the tango in 4. The tango forces the fandango to be in 3 and the paso doble to be in 5, which fixes the positions of multiple items, of which the orange costumes are correct in 3 and Terry is correct in 4. The items from (7) can now only fit with Will in 1, turquoise in 2, and June in 3. Of the dances, only the cha-cha can be correct in 1. From (1), the salsa isn't in 6, so it's in 2. Mork is below the salsa, but can't be correct in 5, so he's in 3. Of the wives, Betty or Grace could be correct, but since from (3) Betty isn't in 1, Grace must be correct in 6. That places Betty in 4, and since the green costume is above Betty, it's in 1. Everything else can be placed by elimination.

8 Identity Parade 1

A   B   C   D

From (1), mouth A is on face B or C, and from (3), mouth C is on face A or B, so neither is correct. If mouth B is correct, then mouths A and C are on faces C and A and mouth D must also be correct; this can't be, so mouth B isn't correct and mouth D is. From (1), if hair B were correctly on face B, eyes D would be correctly on face D, but from (2), either hair C or eyes C must be correctly on face C, making two correct features in one of those rows. So hair B is on face A, mouth A is on face B, and eyes D are on face C. With those features placed, eyes C must be on face B, with hair C on face C and nose D on face A (from clue 2); and mouth C must be on face A, with nose C on face C (from clue 3). The only spot remaining for mouth B is on face C. No eyes are yet correctly positioned, so eyes A are on face A and eyes B on face D. All other rows have one correct item, so hair D is on face B and hair A on face D; and nose A is on face B and nose B on face D.

30 Penalty Shootout

The penalty takers' order is DEAFB, and the goalkeeper's order is DACFB. The strikers aimed no penalty kicks at area C, so whenever the goalkeeper dived to that area, a goal must have scored. Only the second and third kicks scored, so that dive was on the second or third kick. Since the first kick did not score, the goalkeeper's first area must match the kickers'. The goalkeeper never dived to E, and didn't dive to B or F first. The kickers aimed at E sometime before A, so the first area was D. The goalkeeper's order, then, is DACFB or DCAFB. Kicks 1, 4, and 5 match the goalkeeper's dives, so the kickers' order is D??FB. Only two slots remain for E and A, and E preceded A, so their order is DEAFB. The third kick scored, so the goalkeeper didn't dive to A on that kick, so the goalkeeper's order is DACFB.

18 The Principal's Cadillac

Clod spray-painted the principal's Cadillac. Since two statements are false, four are true, and the culprit must be mentioned in the four true statements but not the two lies. Only Clod is mentioned four times, so he must be the culprit.

27 Citizen's Arrest

	Citizen's first name	Citizen's last name	Culprit's nickname	Culprit's real name
1	Lesley	Ling	Slasher	Doug
2	Wes	Daffyds	Chopper	Rolf
3	Andy	Jitsoo	Razor	Chesney
4	Colin	Hook	Brutal	Baz
5	Joe	Fitt	Desperate	Sid

From (2), if Jitsoo were in 1, Baz would be correct in 2 and Desperate would be 3. If Baz were correct, Chesney couldn't also be correct in 3, but in the other available positions per (5), Baz would be blocking Chesney in 2, and as for Chesney being in 4, Chopper would then be blocked in 3 by Desperate, leaving no arrangement that works. Jitsoo, then, is in 2 or 3. If Chopper were correct in 3, Chesney in 4 would block Baz, forcing Baz to be in 3 with Desperate correct in 4—but that would make two correct nicknames, so Chopper is in 1 or 2. But from (3), Chopper can't be in 1, so Chopper is in 2 with Chesney correct in 3 and Colin in 4. That eliminates one of Baz's possible positions, forcing Baz to be in 4 with Jitsoo correct in 3 and Desperate in 5. From (3), Lesley is in 1, and from (4), so is Doug. From (4), Andy and Fitt are either in 2 and 4 respectively, or 3 and 5. But Fitt can't be correct at 4 since Jitsoo is already correct in that column, so Andy is in 3 and Fitt in 5. Only Wes can be correct in his column, so he's in 2 and Joe is in 5. The only nickname that can be correct is Slasher, so Slasher is in 1. From (1), Razor must be in 3 and Hook in 4, and everything else can be determined by elimination.

56 Safe Cracker 9

The combination is 8475.

21 Counting Sheep 2

9		5	3		3
2	8	8			2
1		4	7	8	
8	5			1	6
	2		6	3	9
	5	3	4	8	

35 Boxing Clever

	Nickname	Real name	Knockout punch	Winning round
1	Killer	Mike	uppercut	1
2	Sugar	Sid	left jab	5
3	Basher	Joe	hook	3
4	Iron	Bloggs	right jab	7
5	Hitman	Roy	body shot	4
6	Lightning	Henry	straight	8

From (3), Basher is in 2, 3, or 4, and from (6) Hitman is in 3, 4, or 5. But according to (4), Basher and Hitman are not adjacent. Basher, therefore, cannot be in 4 (or Hitman would have to be adjacent in 3 or 5), and, similarly, Hitman cannot be in 3. Basher and Hitman cannot be adjacent in 3 and 4, nor can they both be correct in 2 and 5, so they are either in 2 and 4 or in 3 and 5 respectively. If they were in 2 and 4, from (7) Mike would have to be in 3. (If he were in 2, the right jab would be correct at 5, but the body shot would already be correct at 4, two below Basher.) But then there is no set of three consecutive empty slots in the last name, winning round, and knockout punch columns for the items from (2). Basher, then, is in 3, with Hitman correct in 5. Of the associated items, round 8 is correct in 6. Because round 8 is correct, round 5 cannot also be correct, so of the items from (7), Mike is correct in 1, round 5 is in 2, and the right jab is in 4. There is only one placement for the items from (2): Bloggs is in 4, round 4 is in 5, and Lightning is in 6. From (5), the left jab must be in 2 and round 1 in 1. Now only the straight punch can be correct in 6, so the uppercut is in 1. From (1), Sugar is one above Joe, but can't be correct in 4, so Sugar is in 2 and Joe is in 3. The rest can be determined by elimination.

6 The Plumber's Apprentice

A controls D, B controls A, C controls B, and D controls C. Tap D can be controlled by either A or B. If it is A, the possibilities are A→D, B→A, C→B, D→C; A→D, B→C, C→A, D→B; or A→D, B→C, C→B, D→A. If it is B, then we have A→B, B→D, C→A, D→C. Only for the first case is condition 3 satisfied.

12 Card Sharp

The first and third cards are true, and the second and fourth are false. Consider the first card; it and the card below it are the only two cards with at least two cards below them. For the first card to be false, both of those two cards would have to be true—but since it's one of those two cards itself, that can't be, so the first card is true, which means the second card must be false and there must be at least one more true card. If the third card were false, the fourth card would have to be the additional true card; if the third card were true, then the fourth card would have to be false (so the cards would correctly alternate between true and false). In either case, there are two true and two false cards, which means there are not more true statements than false ones, so the fourth card must be false and the third card is true.

42 Pies and Lies

Casey and Tracey ate the pies. Two helpers will always whisper the correct names to Mama Pip, as will two rebels; one helper and one rebel will always whisper the incorrect names. Since there were exactly two correct statements, those must come from one pair of two helpers and one pair of two rebels, which between them must account for all four siblings. The only two pairs which contain all four siblings are Casey and Tracey, and Macey and Stacey. Of the other two pairs, one rebel appeared with both helpers; Tracey is the only sibling in both those pairs, so Casey and Tracey are the rebels.

39 Time and Temperature

The order of days (with temperatures) is Tuesday, 72; Thursday, 60; Friday, 48; Sunday, 46; Saturday, 44; Wednesday, 42; Monday, 33.

First we must find the order of days. For brevity, we'll refer to a day by its first two letters (e.g., Thursday is TH). from (3) and (6), WE, FR, and SU are either (i) FR SU – WE, (ii) SU FR WE, or (iii) FR SU WE. From (2), there is one day between SA and MO. If (ii) or (iii) are the case, that day must be TU or TH, and whichever it is, from (4) the other one is no more than two days away. Given those constraints, it's impossible to get TU far enough from MO to fulfill (5), so (i) above is correct. Since we've shown that neither TU or TH can go between SA and MO, WE must be between them, making FR SU SA WE MO. From (5), TU must precede that sequence, and from (4), to stay close enough to TU, TH also must precede the sequence. From (1), TH can't be first or it would be too far from WE, so the final sequence is TU TH FR SU SA WE MO.

As for part two, the days in order are Tuesday, Thursday, Friday, Sunday, Saturday, Wednesday, and Monday with word lengths of, respectively, 7, 8, 6, 6, 8, 9, and 6. For convenience, call the day with the highest temperature D1, down to D7 for the lowest. The possible temperatures from (1) are $D2=42$, $D3=48$, $D4=48$, $D5=54$, and $D6=48$; from (2), they are $D2=39$, $D3=42$, $D4=42$, $D5=45$, and $D6=42$; and from (3), they are $D1=25$; $D2=32$; $D3=40$; $D4=46$; $D5=52$; $D6=60$; $D7=69$. Of the values for (3), D1, D2, and D3 aren't possible since they're lower than all possibilities from (1) and (2) that follow them, and D5, D6, and D7 aren't possible since they're higher than all possibilities from (1) and (2) that precede them. D4, then, is 46. From (1), the only possible value remaining is $D3=48$. From (2), two possible values remain: $D5=45$ or $D6=42$. But from (5) the minimum difference between adjacent temperatures is 2, so D5 isn't 45, so D6 is 42. From (5), D7 is a number from 30 to 40. From (4), it can't be 40, because $4 \times 2 \times 4 \times 0 = 0$. So we know three of the digits of the product are 4, 2, and 3; since $4 \times 2 \times 3 = 24$, either D1 or D2 is a product of 24. That product isn't 48, since D3 is 48. But from (5), the maximum difference between D1 and D3 is 24, so D1 can't be higher than 72. Therefore 72 is the product from (4), and D7 is 33. D2 must be 60 (anything else would have a difference greater than 12 with either D1 or D3), and since from (5) the minimum difference between adjacent temperatures is 2, D5 is 44.

15 Alien Mutations 2

A: head becomes square; B: add antennae; C: body becomes circular; D: remove lower appendages; E: body becomes square; F: posture becomes upright; G: posture becomes horizontal; H: add upper appendages; I: remove antennae.

46 Crime Wave

	Title	Surname	Location	Weapon
1	Professor	Indigo	shed	hammer
2	Earl	Blew	attic	acid
3	Lord	Mauve	basement	dynamite
4	Doctor	Tomato	bathroom	poker
5	Sir	Carrot	playroom	blowtorch
6	Duchess	Grey	greenhouse	cyanide

From (4), the professor is in 1–3; from (2) and (6), the earl and lord are in 1–4. From (6) and (7), the lord cannot be one place higher than the professor or earl. From (4) and (6), the lord cannot be one place lower than the professor (because the bathroom is three places below the professor and the playroom is two below the lord). The lord cannot be in 2, then. If the professor were in 2 with the bathroom correct in 5, the lord couldn't be in 1 or 3, so would be in 4, but then the playroom would also be correct in 6, so that can't be the case either. There are now two possible arrangements of the professor, earl, and lord: the lord in 1, the professor in 3, and the earl in 4; or the professor correct in 1, the earl in 2, and the lord in 3. In the former arrangement, the poker is in 2, the playroom in 3, Tomato in 6, and the bathroom in 6. If we then try to place the items in (3) and (5), we find only one available position for each, but those two positions conflict, placing both Grey and Mauve in 4. So the latter arrangement is correct; of the other items placed, Tomato and the poker are correct in 4. The items in (3) can only be placed with the shed correct at 1. From (5), dynamite is in 3 and Grey in 6. The blowtorch can't also be correct in 1, but from (1) it cannot be in the lowest space on the list, so it's in 5 and the greenhouse and duchess are both in 6. None of the remaining last names can be placed correctly, and from (8) Indigo can't be in the lowest available spot, so Indigo is in 1, and the remaining items can all be placed by elimination.

6 Treasure Chests

If A contained the treasure, only chest D's statement would be false. If B contained the treasure, only chest A's statement would be true. Since neither A nor B contains the treasure, chest A's statement is false and B's and D's are true. That means C's statement must be false, so chest C contains the treasure.

21 Safe Cracker 3

The combination is 6425.

23 Alien Mutations 3

A: remove rear appendages; B: head becomes square; C: posture becomes upright; D: remove antennae; E: add antennae; F: remove lower appendages; G: body becomes circular; H: add lower appendages; I: posture becomes horizontal; J: remove upper appendages; K: body becomes square; L: head becomes circular.

60 Holmes's Sweet Home

Benjamin broke the window. Consider the four combinations of truth (T) and falsehood (F) for the two statements each is faced with: TT, TF, FT, and FF. Then consider how each would answer if he or she were uttering truthfully or falsely. For Catherine a "no" means the first statement is true and a "yes" means it is false, whereas for both Daniel and Florence, a "yes" means the first statement is true and a "no" means it is false. Since one answer was different from the others, we can eliminate as a suspect anyone who would be implicated by three "yes" or three "no" answers. If Catherine, Daniel, and Florence all answered "yes"—implying the first questions put to them were false, true, and true, respectively—the suspects (listed by initial) would be CD, BCD, and CD; for the opposite responses, the suspects would be ABEF, AEF, and ABEF, respectively. The only suspect who does not appear solely among one of those sets is Benjamin (and Catherine, Daniel, and Florence's answers were "no," "yes," and "no," respectively).

24 Eggs Dream Logic Puzzle

The final order is: 1st, George; 2nd, Frank; 3rd, Cathy; 4th, Dave; 5th, Ethel; 6th, Bernie; and 7th, Alan. The table shows the restrictions on the final positions as given by conditions 1–4 and 6–8, where an × represents an eliminated cell.

	1	2	3	4	5	6	7
A	×	×	×	×			
B				×	×		×
C				×	×	×	×
D	×		×				
E				×			×
F	×		×	×			
G			×				

If Cathy is not in the top three then she has no other place to finish, so she must be in the top three. Therefore, from (5), Ethel and Bernie must be outside the top three, so we can × out B1, B2, B3, E1, E2, and E3. Bernie can now only be sixth, and if we × out the remaining cells in that column, only one cell remains in row E; continuing similarly, we find the remaining placements by elimination.

40 Apart Meant

1: Jim; 2: Dave; 3: Amy; 4: Sally; 5: Tina; 6: Bob. Since a female is in 5, note (a) can't be on door 2. If note (a) were on door 1, Tina would have to be in 5, with note (e) on door 6. But with Bob in 4 and Tina in 5, Sally would be in 6, meaning both notes (e) and (f) were on door 6, which can't be. Therefore, note (a) is on door 3 and Bob is in 6. If Sally were in 5 with Tina in 4, we would again have notes (e) and (f) on the same door, so Sally is in 4 and Tina is in 5. Note (f) is on door 4 and note (e) is on door 6, so note (d) is on door 5 and Dave or Jim lives in 2. Note (b) can't be on door 1 since the only apartment it's next to is occupied by a man, and note (a) is already on door 3, so note (b) is on door 2, leaving door 1 as the only spot for note (c). Jim, then, lives in 1, which means Amy lives in 3 and Dave is in 2.

13 The Six Window Cleaners

The order, from highest to lowest, was Doris, Bert, Alf, Freda, Colin, and Ethel.

25 Safe Cracker 4

The combination is 5942.

51 Talent Ted

	First name	Last name	Act	Items used
1	Alf	Bloggs	smashing	flowers
2	Dee	Arted	throwing	plates
3	Fred	King	juggling	bottles
4	Carol	Singer	waving	carrots
5	Joe	Looded	spinning	knives
6	Peter	Hout	eating	eggs

From (5), Fred is in 1, 2, or 3; if Fred were correct in 1, eating would be in 4. Dee then couldn't be correct in 3, and from (2) would have to be in 2, but that would place waving in 4 as well, so Fred is not in 1. From (2), Dee is in 1, 2, or 3; if Dee were in 3, waving would be in 5. Fred would then be in 2, but that would place eating in 5 as well, so Dee is not in 3. If Fred were in 2, Dee would be in 1, placing waving and eating at 3 and 5 respectively. Both those positions are correct, which can't be, so Fred is not in 2 and is in 3 with carrots correct in 4 and eating in 6. From (6), Carol is either in 2 or 4. If Carol were in 2, spinning would be in 3, but then there's no way to resolve (2), since either Dee would need to occupy 2, where Carol is, or waving would need to occupy 3, where spinning is. So Carol isn't in 2 and is in 4, with bottles in 3 and spinning in 5. Plates aren't also correct in 1, so from (1) they must be in 2 with Singer in 4. That leaves only one position for the items in (2): Dee in 2, waving in 4, and Looded in 5. Of the remaining acts, only throwing can be correct, in 2. From (4), the flowers must be in 1, juggling in 3, and Hout in 6. From (3), Alf is one place from Arted, so Alf can't be in 5 or 6; Alf, then, is in 1 and Arted in 2. Joe and Bloggs must be correct in the first two columns in 5 and 1, respectively. Other placements can be determined by elimination.

22 Logical Line

The order was Barbara, Frank, George, Connie, Edward, David, Alice. To be symmetric, there must be a girl at the center. There must also be an equal number of boys and an equal number of girls on either side of the center. So the possible distributions of boys (B) and girls (G) are as follows: (a) GBBGBBG, (b) BGBGBGB, or (c) BBGGGBB. From (1), there are two boys to the left of Alice. Adding condition (2) means that there are at least three boys to the left of Alice, so distribution (c) does not apply. So we have these two options:

(a) G	B	B	G	B	B	Alice
(b) Frank	G	Edward	G	David	Alice	George

However, since, from clue (3), Connie is to the right of George, (b) does not work and we are left with (a). Connie cannot be the first girl if she is to the right of George, so she must be the middle one with Barbara the leftmost:

Barbara	B	B	Connie	B	B	Alice

From (1) and (2), Frank is to the left of Edward and George, and David is to the right of Edward, so Frank is the leftmost boy.

Barbara	Frank	B	Connie	B	B	Alice

From (3), Connie is to the right of George, so George is the boy between Frank and Connie. As for the two remaining boys, from (1) we know that David is to Edward's right, so the final arrangement must be:

Barbara	Frank	George	Connie	Edward	David	Alice

31 Alien Mutations 4

A: add antennae; B: add upper appendages; C: remove lower appendages; D: posture becomes horizontal; E: remove antennae; F: head becomes circular; G: head becomes circular; H: body becomes circular; I: body becomes square; J: body becomes circular; K: add antennae; L: posture becomes upright.

Arthur owns the frog in Helsinki, Benny owns the cat in Paris, Cathy owns the goat in London, Doris owns the elephant in Berlin, and Eve owns the dog in New York. The diagram below shows the first set of deductions that can be made from the clues.

	cat	dog	elephant	frog	goat	Berlin	Helsinki	London	New York	Paris
Arthur			X						X	X
Benny		X		X		X				
Cathy	X	X		X		X	X			X
Doris	X						X	X		
Eve				X						
Berlin	X									
Helsinki										
London			X							
New York	X		X		X					
Paris			X							

The New York owner must own either the dog or frog, and neither Benny nor Cathy owns the dog or frog, so neither lives in New York. This leaves only Eve as the owner in New York, and Eve doesn't own the frog, so she owns the dog. Cathy can now only be in London, and she owns either the elephant or goat. The elephant isn't in London, so she owns the goat.

The elephant is owned by Benny or Doris (who, if she does not own the elephant, owns the frog) in either Berlin or Helsinki. Benny can be in Helsinki or Paris, whereas Doris can be in Berlin or Paris. Two possibilities now arise: (a) the elephant is owned by Benny in Helsinki, or (b) it is owned by Doris in Berlin. If (a) is the case, Doris must own the frog in Paris, but then Arthur would have to be in Berlin with the cat, and the cat owner must live in either Helsinki or Paris, so (b) must be the case, and the elephant is owned by Doris in Berlin. Paris can now only have Benny who can only have the cat, leaving the frog in Helsinki with Arthur.

28 Safe Cracker 5

The combination is 9543.

53 Gone Away

	First name	Last name	Destination	Days
1	Dave	Castaway	Corfu	12
2	Freddie	Monk	Rome	14
3	Connie	Idle	Tenerife	7
4	Ethel	Drip	Barcelona	5
5	Arthur	Wise	Ibiza	10
6	Barbara	Rich	Menorca	4

From (2), (4), (5), and (6), Corfu and Rome must be in 1, 2, or 3, and Tenerife and Barcelona must be in 2, 3, or 4. So those four destinations account for all four slots, and additionally either Corfu or Rome must be in 1, while Tenerife or Barcelona must be in 4. From (6), if Rome were in 3, Idle would be in 4. But then Corfu would have to be in 1, which, from (2), would place Drip in 4 as well, so that's not possible. From (4), if Barcelona were in 2, Barbara would be in 4, but then Rome could only be in 1, in which case, from (6), Arthur would also have to be in 4, so that can also be eliminated. From (5), if Tenerife were in 2 with the 10-day vacation correct in 4, then Barcelona would have to be the destination in 4, but that would make the 7-day vacation also correct in 3, so Tenerife isn't in 2, which means Corfu and Rome are in 1 and 2 in some order, and Barcelona and Tenerife are in 3 and 4 in some order. Thus, from (5) and (6), Monk and Idle must be in 2 and 3 in some order. Monk's position is tied to Tenerife and Idle's to Rome, so destinations 1–4 must either be Rome/Corfu/Barcelona/Tenerife or Corfu/Rome/Tenerife/Barcelona. In the former arrangement, Connie, Arthur, and Barbara would end up in 2, 4, and 5 and the 7-day, 4-day, and 10-day vacations in 2, 5, and 6—but that leaves nowhere for Freddie and the 12-day vacation from (1) to fit, so it's the latter, where Freddie fits into position 2 and the 12-day vacation in position 1. The remainder can be placed by elimination.

11 Unchained Melody

The singers were A, B, G, and H. Prisoner D can hear two of A, E, and G. However, since B only hears one of A, C, or E, and H only hears one of E, G, or I, then D hears A and G. No column has three singers so D is not one of them. Prisoner C can hear one of B or F, and I can hear one of F or H. This means that E can only hear B and H.

28 Magic Hats 2

Ant wears a black hat, Bendy wears a black hat, Cringe wears a white hat, and Dodgy wears a black hat. There are two liars: Bendy and Dodgy. If Bendy were wearing a white hat, then he would be truthfully reporting seeing two white hats and one black hat. That would mean there were only one black hat worn among the four friends, in which case Ant's and Cringe's statement could not be true. To make untrue statements, they would both need to wear black hats, creating a contradiction. So Bendy's hat is black. By the same reasoning, so is Dodgy's hat. Cringe's statement, therefore, is true. If Cringe's hat were black, Ant's statement would be false—but there are only three black hats, so there is no fourth black hat for Ant to wear. Cringe's hat, then, is white, and Ant's statement is true. If Ant's hat were white, then both Bendy's and Dodgy's statements would be true, contradicting the fact that at least one statement is a lie. So Ant's hat is black, and Bendy and Dodgy are both lying.

52 The Singing Citizen

The singing citizen in is house #8. Since the culprit is a honest citizen and honest citizens always tell the truth, the culprit's statement must list his or her own house number. Only two interviewees' statements fit that description: 2 and 8. The three criminals must be the three who did not mention the culprit. For 2, they are 1, 5, and 8; for 8, they are 2, 4, and 9. Houses 5 and 8 are in the same column, however, and we know no two criminals live in the same row or column, so 8 is the culprit with the criminals in houses 2, 4, and 9.

34 False Friend

Dan stole Officer Whistle's hat. Consider a pair of friends involved in the whispering and reporting. If one of that pair is the liar, that person's name can never be mentioned as a suspect. However, in (1) Andrea is reported, in (2) Elizabeth is reported, in (3) Frank is reported, and in (6) Connie is reported. So these can be eliminated, leaving Brian or Dan as the liar. If Brian were the liar, then in (1) Andrea and Dan as truth-tellers would have reported him to the officer, but he is not mentioned. Therefore Dan is the liar and thief.

38 Alien Mutations 5

A: add lower appendages; B: posture becomes upright; C: body becomes square; D: posture becomes horizontal; E: remove upper appendages; F: remove antennae; G: add antennae; H: body becomes square; I: body becomes circular; J: remove upper appendages; K: head becomes circular; L: posture becomes horizontal.

47 Ranking Officers

The four jeeps, in their order of arrival, were taken by the sergeant, general, major, and captain. From (1) and (5), the general didn't take jeep 1 or 3, and the corporal didn't take jeep 2 or 4. From (4), the officers in jeeps 2 and 4, in some order, must have been either the general and captain or the colonel and sergeant. That means the officer who took jeep 3 can't have been either the captain or the sergeant, because from (3) they weren't in consecutive jeeps, and if the captain took jeep 3, then the sergeant took either jeep 2 or 4 and vice versa. With those options eliminated, from (2) we can eliminate the colonel, major, and corporal as options for jeep 1, leaving the captain and sergeant. Since one of the two took jeep 1, the other can't have taken jeep 2, so we can eliminate them both as options for jeep 2, and the general and colonel as options for jeep 4, leaving the captain and sergeant as the only options for jeep 4 as well. From (5), the sergeant must have taken jeep 1 and the colonel took jeep 4, so from (2) and (4), the general took jeep 2 and the major took jeep 3.

10 Orange County Conundrum

Arthur was mentioned as a suspect twice, Benny twice, Carol three times, Dave twice, and Ethel once. Whoever is guilty, anyone who didn't mention that person as a suspect at all must be a liar. Since there are exactly two liars, the true guilty party must have been named three times; therefore, Carol took the carrots and Carol and Ethel were lying.

58 Safe Cracker 10

The combination is 7459.

45 Alien Mutations 6

A: add antennae; B: posture becomes horizontal; C: head becomes square; D: remove upper appendages; E: body becomes circular; F: posture becomes upright; G: posture becomes upright; H: add lower appendages; I: remove lower appendages; J: head becomes circular; K: body becomes square; L: remove antennae.

48 Corridor Conundrum

If there are three liars in the corridor and only two incorrect doors, at least two of the liars must name the same incorrect door number. The pleasure-seeker then knows that this number is incorrect and that the guard on this door is a liar. Let's assume door 3 was given as an answer twice by the corridor guards. When the pleasure-seeker reaches the room, he has one of two options. He can ask the guard in front of door 3 (who he knows to be a liar), "Does this door lead to eternal happiness?" while pointing to either door 1 or door 2. If the guard responds "no" then the door pointed to is the correct one; if he responds "yes" then it is the other door of the two. Alternately, he could ask the guard in front of either door 1 or door 2, "Does this door lead to eternal happiness?" while pointing to door 3 (which he knows is not the case). If the guard responds "no" then that guard is a truth-teller and is guarding the correct door; if he responds "yes" then he is a liar and the other door of the two is correct.

19 Fine Felines

	First name	Last name	Cat	Prize
1	Ben	Doon	Lucy	potatoes
2	Des	Ninall	Oggy	teabags
3	Cath	Holick	KP	sausages
4	Eve	Brain	Nellie	deodorant
5	Arthur	Parrot	Minnie	aspirin

From (5), Doon is either at 1 or 2. If Doon were correctly at 2, sausages would also be correct at 4. If Doon were correct, Holick couldn't be, so from (3), Holick would be at 1—but that puts aspirin correctly at 3, which also can't be the case, so Doon is at 1, with sausages at 3 and Nellie correctly at 4. Minnie can't also be correct, so from (2), Minnie is at 5 and Cath is correct at 3. From (3), Eve can now only be at 4, with Holick correctly at 3 and aspirin at 5. No prize is correctly placed yet; from (4), deodorant can't be correctly placed at 2, so potatoes is correct at 1. Everything else can be placed by elimination, including choices ruled out by (1) and (4).

56 Key Caper

The order was Ben, Ella, Carrie, Alan, Danae, Francis. Considering who B can pass the key to, and who those people could pass to, the block of four consecutive students that starts with B might be BECA, BECD, BFAC, BFAD, or BFEC. Those groups could continue to BECAD, BECAF, BECDF, BFACD, BFADE, or BFECA. The sequence BECAF isn't possible because the only missing member of the sequence is D, and D is not one of the people F could pass the key to; as for BECDF, it could continue to A, but B is not one of the people A could pass the key to, so the sequence could not loop. The other four sequences are possible, however, giving us BECADF, BFACDE, BFADEC, or BFECAD. In the correct sequence, F must follow A. All the possible rotations of those sequences in which F follows A are BECADF, ECADFB, CADFBE, ADFBEC, ACDEBF, ADECBF, ECADBF, CADBFE, and ADBFEC. We can eliminate any sequences in which A is first or second or in which B is fifth or sixth, which leaves only one possible sequence: BECADF.

20 Careless Whispers

The correct closing time was 4 P.M. There are three possible combinations of the liar (L) and two truth-tellers (T_1 and T_2): LT_1, LT_2, or T_1T_2. The first two combinations produce incorrect information while the last gives correct information. So we know there are two false answers and one true answer. This table shows the possible closing times assuming each answer is true or false:

statement	if true	if false
1	2, 4, 6, 8	1, 3, 5, 7, 9
2	2, 3, 5, 6, 7, 8	1, 4, 9
3	2, 3, 5, 7	1, 4, 6, 8, 9

The answer must appear in one true and two false options; only 4 P.M. satisfies that condition.

33 Counting Sheep 3

	8	2		3	7
7	1	8	4		
6		3		2	9
3	9		5		3
4		7	3	6	
	2		8	9	1

44 Safe Cracker 7

The combination is 9132.

50 Alien Mutations 7

A: body becomes square; B: body becomes circular; C: head becomes circular; D: add antennae; E: head becomes square; F: posture becomes horizontal; G: add upper appendages; H: posture becomes upright; I: remove lower appendages; J: posture becomes upright; K: add antennae; L: body becomes circular; M: posture becomes horizontal; N: remove antennae; O: remove lower appendages; P: add lower appendages.

14 Birthday Brainbuster

Agatha has a birthday in July, Bibble in April, Crump in August, and Dibdib in January. Either: (a) Agatha lies, Bibble is truthful, Crump is truthful, and Dibdib lies; or (b) Agatha is truthful, Bibble lies, Crump lies, and Dibdib is truthful. For case (a), we have the following true statements: (i) At least one letter in Agatha's month appears in Bibble's, (ii) Bibble's month is later than Dibdib's in the calendar, (iii) Crump's month has 31 days, (iv) Dibdib's month has 31 days. For case (b), the opposites of statements (i)–(iv) above hold. Only four series of four consecutive numbers are possible: 3–6, 4–7, 5–8, and 6–9. For each series we can list the possible months under each of the four numbers together with the number of days in each month and check statements (i)–(iv) against the list, remembering that Agatha is the first number, Bibble the second, and so on. All four series must be tested against (i)–(iv) for both cases (a) and (b). Only for case (a) and series 4–7 is there a set of months for which (i)–(iv) hold true.

26 Saw Point

Let us label the machines A, B, C, and D. Inside the room, two of the machines are switched off—let's say B and C, leaving A and D on. Outside the room, let us label the switches E, F, G, and H. All six combinations of two switches are tripped until no sound can be heard. Let's say the two "on" switches are E and G. So the switches E and G correspond in some order to the machines that are off (B and C), while F and H correspond with A and D in some order. While still outside the room, turn one of the "on" switches off, say E (leaving switch G on), and turn one of the "off" switches on, say F (leaving H off). Inside the room, a single machine will be running, say D, and that will correspond to switch F (the "off" switch that was turned on), so machine A must correspond to H. Now flick the switches of B and C to see which one turns on. Say B is the one that turns on; that means B corresponds to G (the "on" switch that wasn't turned off), leaving C and E as the last pair. (This puzzle is an improved version of a puzzle of mine that first appeared in *Brain Busters*.)

20 See-Saw Sums

Of the last pair, one must weigh twice the other, so the second balance must include (referring to friends by weight ratios) 1 and 2, 2 and 4, or all three of those. Thus, the possible second balances are (a) 1, 2, and 4: $(1\times2)+(2\times1)=(4\times1)$; (b) 1, 2, and 5: $(2\times2)+(1\times1)=(5\times1)$; (c) 2, 3, and 4: $(3\times2)+(2\times1)=(4\times2)$; and (d) 2, 4, and 5: $(4\times2)+(2\times1)=(5\times2)$. For (c), there is no possible first weighing. For (b) and (d), 5 must climb off next, but 5 isn't lighter than anyone, so the second balance is (a). The only possible first balance, then, is $(2\times2)+(5\times1)=(1\times1)+(4\times2)$ with 3 omitted, so 1 climbed off second.

29 Wed Luck

Gina & Larry married in Atlanta; Ethel & Ian married in Boston; Harriet & Keith married in Columbus; and Freda & Jim married in Denver. The given clues eliminate the following possibilities:

	Ethel	Freda	Gina	Harriet	Ian	Jim	Keith	Larry
Atlanta	✕					✕	✕	
Boston		✕					✕	✕
Columbus		✕						
Denver							✕	
Ian		✕						
Jim								
Keith	✕		✕					
Larry		✕						

Keith can only have married in Columbus. Keith married either Freda or Harriet, but Freda did not marry in Columbus, so he married Harriet. By elimination, Freda married Jim, and they can only have married in Denver. The remaining pairings can be determined by elimination.

7 Pet Peeve

	Owner's first name	Owner's last name	Pet	Pet's name
1	Bess	Lyne	cat	George
2	Jake	Nose	pig	Helen
3	Sid	Crud	rabbit	Josie
4	Alvin	Dank	goat	Ian
5	Trish	Kline	dog	Fred

From (4) Sid can be at 3 or 4, and from (5) Trish can be at 4 or 5. If Sid were at 4, Trish would be at 5, which would mean two first names were correctly positioned, so Sid must be at 3, and from (4), Dank is at 4 and the cat is at 1. From (2), Alvin is at 2 or 4, with Crud at 1 or 3. If Alvin were at 2 and Crud at 1, then from (4), Nose would be at 2 and Trish at 5, again making two correctly positioned first names. Alvin, then, is at 4, Crud is correct at 3, and Fred is at 5. Since 4 is occupied, Trish is correct at 5 and Nose is at 2. Columns 1 and 2 already have one correct item in each, so Jake and Kline aren't at 1; Jake is at 2 with Bess at 1, and Kline is at 5 with Lyne at 1. From (1), Ian can only fit at 4 with the pig at 2, both in correct positions, and from (3) the rabbit and Josie must be at 3. The dog can't also be correct at 4, so it's at 5 with the goat at 4, and George can't be correct at 2, so he's at 1 with Helen at 2.

18 Odd Auditions

Cordelia got the part. At first it seems that we want to know who is ranked first, but there is insufficient information to order the eight names. However, a little lateral thinking reveals that, in one of the possible arrangements of the eight names, the initials spell CORDELIA—the director happened to use an unorthodox method of noting his casting choice.

47 Safe Cracker 8

The combination is 5197.

59 Terrible Tunes

Bob suggested Folly and plays piano, Cindy suggested the Goons and plays bass, Delilah suggested the Muddles and plays drums, Evan suggested Humbug and plays trumpet, and Felicity suggested the Drips and plays the guitar. The diagram below shows what we know from the given clues:

	bass	drums	guitar	piano	trumpet	The Drips	Folly	The Goons	Humbug	The Muddles
Bob						✕				✕
Cindy		✕					✕		✕	✕
Delilah										
Evan	✕	✕		✕		✕		✕		
Felicity	✕	✕		✕				✕		✕
The Drips				✕	✕					
Folly		✕								
The Goons		✕		✕						
Humbug		✕	✕	✕						
The Muddles			✕		✕					

The Muddles was suggested by either Delilah or Evan, but was not suggested by the guitarist or trumpeter. Evan plays either guitar or trumpet, so Delilah suggested the Muddles. Evan and Felicity both play either guitar or trumpet, so none of the other three band members do. The Goons was suggested by Bob or Cindy, and by someone who plays bass, guitar, or trumpet. Evan and Felicity play guitar and trumpet, so the bassist suggested the Goons. By elimination, the trumpeter suggested Humbug. The Drips was suggested by Cindy or Felicity and by the drummer or guitarist. Neither Cindy nor Felicity plays drums, so the guitarist suggested the Drips, and by elimination the drummer suggested the Muddles and the pianist suggested Folly. Neither Cindy nor Delilah suggested Folly and neither Evan nor Felicity plays piano, so Bob suggested Folly and plays piano. By elimination, Delilah plays drums, Cindy plays bass and suggested the Goons, Evan suggested Humbug and thus is the trumpet player, and Felicity suggested the Drips and plays guitar.

32 Brain Food

	First name	Last name	Dish
1	Florence	Hobble	lasagna
2	Arnie	Grunge	macaroni
3	Cathy	Jib	risotto
4	Barbara	Krank	trout
5	Dave	Izzy	omelette
6	Ernie	Lisp	salmon

From (5), if Grunge were correct in 1, trout would be in 3 with Dave correct in 4. But then from (2), Arnie couldn't also be correct in 1; if he were in 2, risotto would be blocked in 3 by trout; and if he were in 3, Krank would be correct in 5, making two correct last names. Grunge is in 2 or 3, then. From (4), if Jib were correct in 4 with Barbara in 5 and omelette in 6, Grunge would be in 3. That blocks two of Krank's four possible positions from (2); Krank also couldn't be in 5 (that would make two correct last names), and in 6, risotto would be blocked by trout from (5). From (3), Jib isn't in 1, so Jib is also in 2 or 3. In either case, trout and omelette are in 4 and 5 in some order. From (2), risotto is one above Krank, so Krank isn't in 5 or 6 and must be in 4 (with risotto in 3 and Arnie in 2). Lisp, then, is the only possible correct last name, so Lisp is in 6. From (3), Florence is above Jib, and whether Jib is in 2 or 3, Florence must be in 1. From (1), Izzy isn't in 1, so Izzy is in 5 and Hobble in 1. Also from (1), Izzy is above Ernie, so Ernie is in 6. Dave, then, can't be in 6, so Grunge isn't in 3; Grunge is in 2 and Jib in 3 (with trout, omelette, Barbara, and Dave placed appropriately; trout's position is correct). From (1), lasagna isn't in 6, and from (3), neither is macaroni, so salmon is in 6. The rest can be placed by elimination.

44 Counting Sheep 4

4	8			1	7
	1	6	4	9	
2		6		3	9
	9	3	5		3
5		5	3	7	
9	2		8		1

41 Mad Movies

	First name	Last name	Movie	Director
1	Bert	Klink	*Eight*	Tapintoono
2	Connie	Howdydo	*Cyclo*	Vastcounti
3	Doris	Jiff	*Ben-Him*	Loser
4	Fred	Grump	*Queen Kang*	Hitchfrock
5	Edgar	Limpet	*Rebuke Her*	Spoolbag
6	Alf	Ink	*Low Midnight*	Einstein

From (3) and (5), if Doris were in 4, Edgar would be in 2. Those positions would place Einstein and Vastcounti in 3, so Doris isn't in 4. If Doris were in 5, Vastcounti would be correct in 4 and *Eight* correct in 3. Hitchfrock couldn't then also be correct in 3, so from (4) he would be in 5—but that places *Rebuke Her* in 6, making two correct movies, so Doris isn't in 5. If Doris were in 6 with Vastcounti in 5 and *Eight* in 4, the trio in (4) could only fit with Howdydo correct in 2, Hitchfrock in 4, and *Rebuke Her* in 5. From (5), Grump couldn't also be correct in 1, nor could Grump be in 3 because Einstein couldn't also be in 5. That leaves 4 for Grump, but then Edgar would be adjacent to Doris, contradicting (5). Doris, then, must be in 3, and Edgar is correct in 5 (and of the other items that can now be placed, Einstein is correct in 6). From (6), Fred can't also be correct in 6, so he's in 4 with Jiff in 3 and *Cyclo* correct in 2. From (4), Hitchfrock can't also be correct in 3, so he's in 4 with Howdydo correct in 2 and *Rebuke Her* in 5. The pair in (2) can now only fit with Tapintoono in 1 and *Ben-Him* in 3. Alf isn't also correct in 1, and from (1) he's not Howdydo in 2, so he's in 6. From (1), Klink isn't Alf in 6, and isn't also correct in 5, so Klink is in 1. The rest can be determined by elimination.

54 Alien Mutations 8

A: body becomes circular; B: head becomes circular; C: add lower appendages; D: remove lower appendages; E: add antennae; F: body becomes square; G: remove upper appendages; H: head becomes circular; I: remove antennae; J: add antennae; K: posture becomes upright; L: body becomes circular; M: head becomes square; N: posture becomes horizontal, O: add upper appendages; P: add antennae.

57 Medic Hate

	First name	Last name	Ailment	Remedy
1	Fay	Jape	heartburn	bloodletting
2	Edward	Shirker	laryngitis	leeches
3	Connie	Complane	influenza	cold bath
4	Andy	Pawlea	gout	frog tears
5	Beryl	Grumble	measles	eye of newt
6	Daniel	Worrie	nosebleed	snake blood

From (1), (3), (5), and (7), laryngitis is one place above Connie, the nosebleed is one place below Beryl, and neither Connie and Beryl nor the laryngitis and nosebleed are adjacent. Beryl and Connie both must be in 2, 3, 4, or 5. If Beryl were in 2 with the nosebleed in 3, there's nowhere to place Connie so the laryngitis isn't adjacent to the nosebleed. Similarly, if Connie is in 5 with laryngitis in 4, there's nowhere to place Beryl that doesn't put the nosebleed next to laryngitis. So Beryl is in 3, 4, or 5 and Connie is in 2, 3, or 4. Connie can't be in 4 and Beryl can't be in 3 without Beryl and Connie being adjacent, so those positions can also be eliminated. From (6), Grumble is in 3, 4, 5, or 6, but since Complane is in 2, 3, or 4 per (4) and Pawlea is in 3 or 4, Grumble cannot be in 3 or 4 or no patient's last name could be correct (since Complane, Pawlea, and Grumble, collectively, would be taking up the three positions held by Shirker, Worrie, and Jape). This means both the cold bath and frog tears have been narrowed down to positions 3 and 4. If frog tears is in 3 and the cold bath is in 4, laryngitis is correct in 1 by (3) and gout is also correct in 5 by (6), which is impossible. Therefore, the cold bath is in 3 and frog tears is correct in 4, which places other items via (3) and (6), including Connie in 3. Beryl, then, is in 5 by (5), which places other items via (7). The items in (4) can now only be placed one way: Complane in 3, Edward in 2, and eye of newt in 5. After placing those items, the only last name that can be correct is Shirker in 2, and the only ailment that can be correct is influenza in 3. From (2), measles aren't in 1, so they're in 5. Andy is above measles but not correct in 1, so he's in 4. Jape is above measles in 1, and leeches are above measles but not correct in 1, so they're in 2. Other placements can be made by elimination.

62 Gift Gaffes

	Recipient	Hotel	Wrapping	Gift
1	Billy	Biltless	turquoise	DVD
2	Aaron	Singletree	orange	TV
3	Fiona	Nights Inn	green	guitar
4	George	Weighaton	silver	phone
5	Eva	Ritzy	blue	computer
6	Des	Marrioff	red	book
7	Cher	Five Seasons	yellow	violin

Clue (5) involves the fewest possible placements, so let's consider that first. If George were in 3 with Singletree in 1 and the book in 5, the TV and phone from (4) could only be in 2 and 4 or 4 and 6 respectively, with turquoise in 1 or 3. From (6), the guitar could only be in 2 or 3 (in 4 it blocks both possible positions of the TV and phone), but 2 isn't possible, because that forces silver and turquoise to both be in 3. So the guitar would be in 3, with the Nights Inn also in 3, silver in 4, and Des in 6. From (7), Fiona could only be in 4, with orange correct in 3 and Weighaton in 5. But then where can Aaron from (1) go? Not anywhere below 4; not in 1, where green would be correct in 2, making two correct wrapping paper colors; and not in 2, where orange blocks green one below him. So George is not in 3.

If George were in 5 with Singletree in 3 and the book in 7, the TV from (4) could be in 2, 3, or 4 with the phone two spaces below it in 4, 5, or 6. From (6), the guitar could be in 1 or 4, but if it were correct in 4, that blocks all placements of the TV and phone except the one in which the phone is also correct at 5, so the guitar would be in 1 with the Nights Inn also in 1, silver in 2, and Des (correct) in 4. But then where can Fiona from (7) go? Not in 1 or 7; not in 2, where the Singletree would block the Weighaton one below her; not in 3, where silver would block orange one above her; and not in 6, where she would be correct, making two correct recipients. So George is not in 5 either and must be in 4, with the Singletree in 2 and the book in 6.

From (6), Des can't be in 5, because the Singletree blocks the Nights Inn three above him, so he's in 6 or 7. If Des were in 7 (with Nights Inn in 4, the guitar in 4, and silver in 5, all correct), then from (4), turquoise could only be in 4. (If it were in 2, the phone would also be correct in 5.) Then, from (1) and (7), position 2 would be the only spot in which either Aaron or Fiona could be placed. So Des must be in 6 with Nights Inn and guitar in 3 and silver in 4. With those items placed, from (4), turquoise must be in 1 with the TV in 2 and the phone in 4. There is now only one way to place the items from (7): orange is in 2, Fiona in 3, and the Weighaton in 4. The items from (1) can only be placed with Aaron in 2, green in 3, and the Ritzy in 5. Of the remaining items, only one in each column can be correct: Eva in 5, the Biltless in 1, yellow in 7, and the violin in 7. From (2) the Marrioff is somewhere above Cher, so the Marrioff is in 6 and Cher in 7. From (3), the computer isn't above blue, so the computer is in 5, as is blue. The last items are placed by elimination.

17 Identity Parade 2

From (2), mouths B and C cannot be on adjacent faces, so they are, in some order, on faces A and C, A and D, or B and D. If they were on A and D, however, no mouth could be correct. Also, from (1), mouth C is not on face A, and from (5), mouth B is not on face D. So either mouths B and C are on faces A and C, or they are on faces B and D. From (1), if C were on face D, eyes C would be correctly on face C, but then from (4), eyes B would have to be correctly on face B, which can't be the case, so mouth B is on face A and mouth C is correctly on face C (which places mouth D on face B and mouth A on face D). From (1), eyes C are on face B, and from (4), eyes B are on face D with hair B on face C. No eyes are yet placed correctly, so eyes A must be on face A, and eyes D on face C. From (5), nose B is correctly placed on face B. Nose A isn't also correct, so from (3), nose A is on face C and hair D is correctly on face D. Everything else can be placed by elimination.

58 Counting Sheep 5

3		6	7	4	
	7	3	2		8
4			8	7	1
5	4			2	9
	8	2	3	7	
8	1	9			2

33 Safe Cracker 6

The combination is 7591.

About the Author

Barry R. Clarke writes enigmas for *The Daily Telegraph*, *Prospect* magazine, and *Brain Games* magazine. His puzzle work has also appeared on BBC television. He holds a master's degree in physics, has published papers on quantum mechanics, and is currently writing an academic book on the history of quantum  physics. Recently, he obtained a Ph.D. in Shakespeare authorship studies, defending his thesis "Francis Bacon's contribution to three Shakespeare plays."

He has won awards as a short-film maker, drawn cartoons for his puzzle books, and written comedy sketches for the BBC and ITV. Being also a talented guitarist, he has one unfulfilled ambition, and that is to record an album of his own music. His favorite artists at this time are Chvrches, Cher Lloyd, and Janet Devlin.